Making Garden
Furniture

MAKING GARDEN FURNITURE

Chris Graham

The Crowood Press

First Published in 1996 by
The Crowood Press Ltd
Ramsbury, Marlborough
Wiltshire SN8 2HR

British Library Cataloguing-in-Publication Data
A catalogue reference for this book is available from the British Library.

ISBN 1 85223 987 5

Picture Credits
All illustrations by the author.
Photographs by Christine Cockayne.

Typefaces used: text, New Baskerville and Garamond; headings, Optima Bold.

Typeset and designed by
D & N Publishing, Ramsbury, Marlborough, Wiltshire

Printed and bound in Great Britain by BPC Books Limited, Aylesbury

CONTENTS

one

Garden Design

We all view the garden with different eyes, each member of the family having his or her own schemes for the space. There are gardeners who want to create a perfect planting scheme and put up a greenhouse, children who want room to play without being told to mind the flowers, visitors who appreciate a pleasant outdoor meal, handymen and women who want a nice big garden workshop, fish fanciers and naturalists desiring a well-placed pond, and so on. We tend to expect a lot from our gardens, big or small, and although it is well known that you cannot please everyone, a little planning will certainly ease some of the problems.

I have to admit to being a novice gardener, although this has not stopped me having big ideas. When I planned my present garden (on reflection to please me rather than anyone else), most of my attention centred around the colour, height and flowering time of the plants. It was not until I stopped frenetically digging new borders, planting, moving and replanting, that I realized how totally I had overlooked the question of garden furniture, particularly seating. The plants were quite at home but I had managed to overlook the people. My spouse loves the garden, not as a gardener but to look at, and with nowhere to sit down this can be a very cursory affair.

With a low boundary down one long side of the garden and no mature plants except those forming a boundary hedge, I also found that I needed to introduce some vertical elements to draw the eye away from the traditional long, thin shape that I had inherited. Although I planted some trees to counter this they were far from maturity, meaning that I also needed something instant to fill the gap. Pergolas, rose pillars and arbours are all perfect for this, as the simple open structure is covered in a foliage screen after about three years. I finally chose to erect a pergola between the house and the garden and, since I live in a rural area, I chose rustic poles made from sweet chestnut, to complement the local mixed hedging and the architecture of the house.

My children also finally persuaded me to incorporate a pond (I had been dreading the work involved) which has been a veritable success with them and with visitors, boasting a variety of wildlife: newts, frogs, toads, dragonflies, damsel flies and numerous aquatic insects. It became clear that siting a bench beside it was a matter of some urgency; a simple bridge was also needed to accommodate the frequent and heavy traffic. A second smaller bench is sited near the flower beds where it is rather sunnier, and a table is planned for next spring.

The front of the house posed the problem of having no open ground available for planting. The solution was a series of seasonally planted containers, to brighten what was in effect a parking space. First of all I tried terracotta, but this was unsuccessful due to the high incidence of accidental damage when parking the cars. I needed something that could fight back! Wooden planters proved ideal, not only could they be made the exact shape of the spaces available, but were sturdy and heavy enough when planted to stand their ground. They also worked out to be extremely economical when compared size for size with ceramic containers, and they are not prone to frost damage.

Because no two gardens are alike, the problems you have will be different from mine. However, you will find that, as your knowledge and skills increase, wood in some form or another can provide a practical and attractive answer. The investment is always negligible in comparison to the cost of ready-made solutions, and should you decide to move you will be able to take most of your work with you.

FURNITURE STYLES

There is a preponderance of moulded plastic furniture in the stores, usually available so cheaply that anyone wishing to host a family meal in the garden feels obliged to succumb. Obviously, you are not one of these, or if you are it is in your past and you bitterly regret it, having found that blinding white is not easy to endure in the mid-summer sun. In deciding to make your own garden furniture, whether it is seating, a table, pergola, arbour or tree house, you have freed yourself and your garden from the tyranny of imposed style and can now choose your own. But which one?

Take advantage of different levels in the garden.

This really depends on your garden, but it may be as well to review the possibilities before you start. Other factors will come into consideration – as well as suiting your garden you will want to suit your pocket, your taste, and your family. I shall start with the furniture.

In Britain, where gardening is a popular leisure activity, perceptions of garden furniture style come mainly from the country house. The designs are loosely based on those of indoor furniture, with the exception of 'rustic' which seems always to have been meant for the garden or summer house. It is likely that garden furniture became distinct from other furniture in the middle of the eighteenth century, before that it was undoubtedly unfashionable to sit or eat outside.

The main styles of garden furniture are represented here by the garden bench; undoubtedly the most necessary and attractive element of garden furnishing.

These styles can be divided into two categories of formal and informal. There is no doubt that the woodland bench is both the easiest to make and the ancestor of all the others – just think of Stonehenge.

WHAT KIND OF GARDEN?

COST

The ultimate cost of the work must take into account timber, tools, hardware and wastage. The first three of these are discussed in later chapters. The latter problem of wastage is bound to be greater with a novice and to some extent is unavoidable. You will, however, begin to save on timber the more you practise.

Do not expect too much of yourself if this is your first experience of joinery; skills have to be learnt. It is much better to begin with a piece on which you have a fair chance of success than to battle away with something over complicated and end up using it for firewood. I know this is in direct contradiction of the current trend for instant gratification and 'easy' accomplishments, but they have a very nasty way of letting you down in the end, and besides this way is much better for your blood pressure.

Moving to a new house is usually the impetus for gardening activity. Very few of us move to a new garden and find as little as I did – usually there is some horrendous bush or badly placed path which urges us to rush out one evening with no more plan than to get rid of it. Sometimes it is an old garden plan of our own, which we have outgrown or become dissatisfied with, that makes us decide to change things.

At this point most of us send for the seed catalogues and raid the local nurseryman for something in flower. I too, have optimistically believed that the pond that I was digging would be fully planted and complete with frogs by Friday, mostly

because I could not stand the idea of having to work so hard for much longer! Impatience and scanty planning usually result in short-lived effects and disappointment, so if there is opportunity for change take some time to think about it.

Lucky gardeners will inherit some hard landscaping: paths, walls, raised beds, arbours, pergolas, decking, perhaps even a bridge. If not then the thoughtful will eschew instant gardening for something more lasting, by installing them themselves. The skills you will need for the woodwork are those of the joiner, and will therefore ensure a lasting demand for your advice and help.

Whether you are planning a new garden or adding to an old scheme, it is important to decide whether it is a formal or informal garden. Informal gardens encompass everything between woodland and a mixed border, but can be generally described as: cottage gardens with or without vegetables, woodland or wild gardens, orchards and some kinds of water features. Formal gardens will have some but not necessarily all of these features: bowling green lawn, clipped hedges, topiary, bedding plants, an herbaceous border with edging stones or strip, an island bed, vistas created by statuary or seating, a summer house or arbour, a pergola, a hard edged pond, a fountain, paved paths (perhaps two, converging) and a patio.

In reality most gardens combine attributes of both formal and informal gardens, the result of trying to squeeze all the amenities into a small plot. The only way to avoid this is to divide the garden into smaller sections. Keeping vegetables at the bottom of the plot, separate from lawn and flower beds, is a familiar example of this. Obviously a rustic seat would look quite wrong in a very formal setting, and a white painted bench would detract from the subtle attractions of a naturalized retreat. Knowing this before you begin will ensure that the time you spend in the workshop is not wasted making something wonderfully unsuitable.

USING YOUR OUTDOOR ROOM

Who uses your garden, and what for, is the ultimate deciding factor in garden and garden furniture design. The different generations often use the space quite differently. Young children need a safe play environment, such as swings over grass or bark chips, a covered sandpit and a play or tree house. They will also want an area for playing ball – although this will not necessarily

A sturdy chair, which suits the stone of the wall.

9

affect your design, it might make an otherwise ideal place for a new bench not so ideal after all. Gardeners will want a shed, greenhouse, compost bin, rose pergolas, pillars or arches, and probably all of them. A disabled gardener would require raised beds, pedestal-leg tables (legs on corners interfere with wheelchairs), ramps for different levels and other adaptations. Given that most families will also want to sit and eat outside, this shows that there is a huge variety of projects to choose from. I shall begin with seating as I believe that this will be the primary consideration.

There are practical and aesthetic considerations in the choice of seating; so far I have only discussed the latter, choice of style and complementing the surroundings. Practical matters include: cost, ability to execute the design and the number of people to be seated.

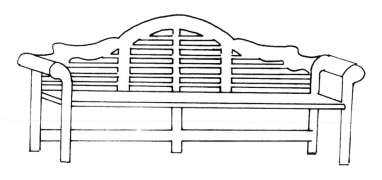

Figure 1 Lutyens bench.

Seating

Now you have what I think is the hardest part, and that is to decide how many people are going to sit down. I can hear you saying 'That's easy, there are only so many of us.' Let me ask you, where are your guests going to sit? 'Which guests?' you answer, 'My mother, my husband's sister and her family, all of them?' Exactly. Just as you cannot hope to seat everyone inside, it cannot be done outside either,

Figure 2 Rustic bench.

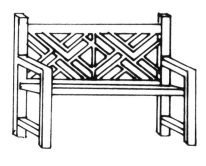

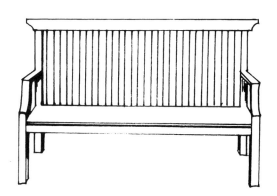

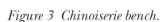

Figure 3 Chinoiserie bench.

unless you want the neighbours to think you have opened a café.

Most of the time I only need one chair in the garden, two is intimate for conversation, six is an open invitation for everyone to join us and bring a snack. Therefore the only answer, I think, is to have two kinds of seating, one where you predominantly eat and talk with friends and one where you predominantly think, or like my spouse, contemplate. Bear in mind that benches can seat up to four, and only involve the same amount of joinery as a single chair.

Figure 4 Edwardian style bench.

Tables

Eating outside can be a very uncomfortable affair. Either it is too hot to do without some kind of canopy, or the table is set just as the first cloud drifts over the face of the sun. Anyone who has eaten outside will also know that white is the most awful colour for a table or cloth as it reflects agonizingly, resulting in diners wearing sunglasses to the table, most unconvivial! This is not a problem with a naturally finished wooden table. People in climates with reliably clement weather adopt the canny and very pretty expedient of placing the table under a pergola or in a gazebo, where the foliage of climbing plants protects them from the midday heat.

Basically we encounter the same problem with tables as we have with seating. If you only want somewhere to place a glass and a sandwich away from the ants, then a small occasional table will do admirably, and will not swamp even the tiniest garden. Family meals will require something more substantial which may not be needed at other times; trestles, folding tables, or a pair of matching tables which can also be sited individually.

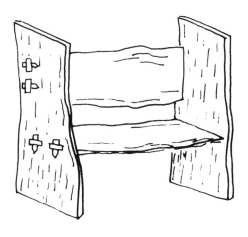

Figure 5 Arts and crafts style bench.

Pergolas, Tunnels, Arches and Arbours

Although these are all really ways of displaying climbing plants, their architecture has an impact even when it is half hidden by mature plants. Wooden constructions in this case are almost invariably the cheapest and once again you are not compromising with someone else's design ideas. Although the idea of a pergola is essentially rather grand, and can use valuable space, a simple choice of timber and construction will make them suitable for more rural surroundings. Arches and tunnels are more difficult to construct due to the shape (arched!), but even a single rose arch over a gate will create an inviting entrance. Siting is the most important element when considering any of the above. Arches, pergolas and tunnels are all meant to be walked under on the way to something; they should cover a path or entrance so that they give the effect both of travelling and arriving. At best they are in an area of heavy traffic so that they are regularly enjoyed. Joining them to the house also makes sense especially if they are overlooked by a window. I have a small pergola, built in a couple of afternoons, which is attached to a wall. It begins at my garden gate and leads to the back door. It is

an excellent addition both to the house and the garden as it seems to join the two together.

Arbours are distinct from other garden structures in that they are self-contained, and may be placed at the junction of two

Curves and arches break up an otherwise boring line.

Fences and panels can be layered to give a sense of depth.

paths or at the end of one. They may contain seats, but are not weatherproof, having an open roof and sides.

Small Structures

The reason for putting a roof over a seat in Britain is obvious; the same goes for adding walls and even a door. The degree of enclosure depends on the purpose of the building, the most weatherproof having the longest season of use. A pavilion usually has only three walls, making it a compromise between a summer house and an arbour, it is a nice place for a small table too, making a cosy retreat. A summerhouse, really a room in the garden, may be pressed into many kinds of service, varying from temporary accommodation to a children's playhouse, or a rather posh garden shed.

Decking Bridges and Planters

Decking can provide an interesting contrast to a lawn and looks good near a pond. I have found that it can be quite slippery in the winter so this is worth bearing in mind when choosing a site. Very few ponds are large enough to need a functional bridge but there is a growing interest in Japanese style gardens, so ornamental bridges are often part of the scheme. As with a pergola, it is just as important that a bridge should lead somewhere, even if it is only leading the eye.

Planters of a reasonable size are increasingly expensive, especially if you want something more sympathetic than plastic. If you stick to one style and size it is a good idea to make more than one of these at a time. You will save time this way and other people are sure to want one when they see yours. Most gardeners could probably fill half a dozen without running out of plants. Wooden planters have obvious drawbacks in that the material will rot in

time, so use a hardwood for maximum longevity. The orange trees at Versailles are grown in wooden containers – incidentally this is the origin of the name 'Versailles box', a very formal design suited to the surroundings of Versailles Palace.

A Versailles box.

two

Seating and Structures

SEATING

Benches

Sometimes fixed seating is preferable, like a bench which surrounds a tree (remember to leave room for the trunk to expand), or a chair at the end of a path. To be in keeping with a Japanese garden, the seating must be low to the ground and, in the spirit of the style, be part of the view. This minimalist approach is often adopted for modern gardens, where a slatted seat might echo decking, or be built into a low retaining wall.

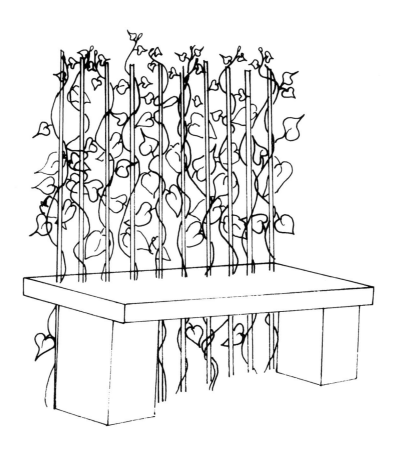

Figure 6 The 'growing' bench.

SEATING

Purpose made seating in a garden has many advantages, the greatest being that it can be designed to complement the setting.

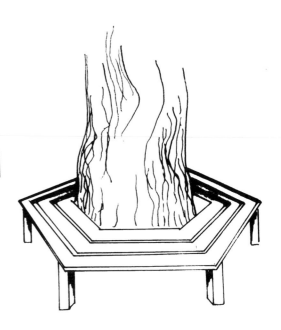

Swinging benches are not for the novice but will be extremely popular with families, the only problem then being who is left standing up! Other novelties include the Growing bench, a variation on the Woodland bench, where the seat is made overwide and large holes are drilled along the back edge to accommodate cane-grown climbers like sweet peas or green beans.

Figure 7 A fixed bench surrounds a tree.

Chairs

Although there is much more work involved if you decide to make chairs instead of a bench, there is no doubt that they do feel different to the sitter. People do not have to share the chair and can sit facing another person for easy conversation. Friends can sit on a bench together, but acquaintances often find it disconcerting.

Chairs with arms are of course the most comfortable and require the most work. All of the really traditional designs have arms, and are therefore more suited to formal surroundings.

To minimize the work involved, armless chairs are

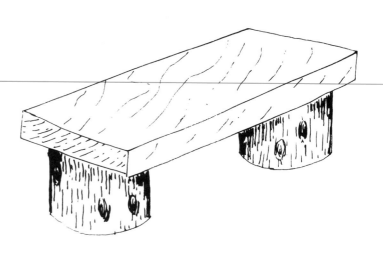

Figure 8 A woodland bench.

to be recommended. They also weigh less, which is a consideration if they are to be moved often. Chairs without backs or arms are stools. Commercially made wooden stools are available so cheaply I will not discuss them further except to mention that small low tables can be made to double as stools and foot stools.

Folding chairs have always been popular for gardens and styles range from functional and charming café-style seating to the deckchair. Advertisements for steamer chairs can be found in many magazines, and though undeniably stylish they are rather complicated to make. Sunbeds with wheels and handles for easy removal to sunny positions have a much simpler construction and look much nicer than their

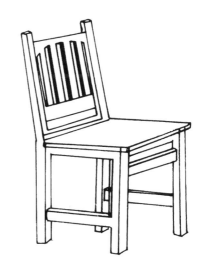

Figure 9 A chair without arms.

Figure 10 A Chinoiserie-style chair with arms.

Figure 11 A folding chair.   *Figure 12 High-backed seat.*

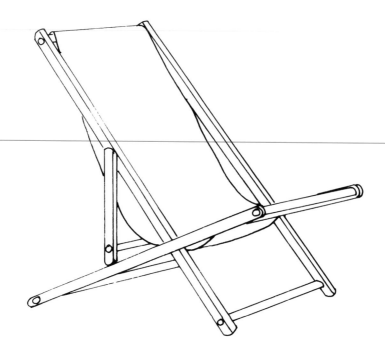

Figure 13 A traditional deckchair.

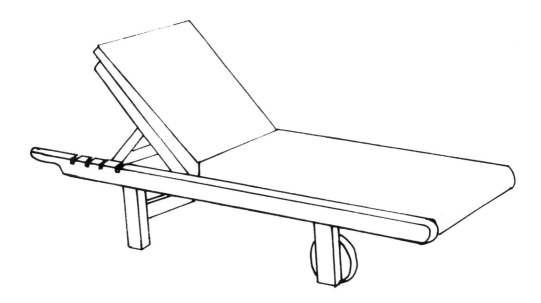

Figure 14 A sunbed with raised section.

mass-produced polycarbonate and steel framed counterparts. Usually it can be arranged so that the head end can be raised and lowered using the same mechanism as a deckchair.

Individual styling of chair components will alter their demeanour considerably. High backs or overlong legs, together with arms, will produce a throne-like seat which you may want to reserve for a special site. Slatted seats can look modern, fragile or sturdily traditional, depending on the colour of the wood, whether it is painted or not, the section used and the construction. So before you begin, plan not only exactly the style, use and siting of your chair, but also the finish you will use.

TABLES

If you are making chairs and a table, then choose one style for them both, just as you would for indoor furniture. As pointed out earlier, to site a full-size dining table can be problematic and may impede traffic to certain areas of the garden. But whatever size is decided upon, the first decision will be about how many legs to have.

Pedestals are especially suited to round-topped tables and make good use of space, as chairs can be pushed well under when not in use, there being no legs to get in the way.

Two supports are usually found on rectangular tables, one at each short end. Although this type of leg can be very elegant it is also eminently suited to tusk tenon construction. A deconstruction of this would be the trestle table, where the top is held on by its weight only. After use the top and legs can be stored separately relatively easily, although this may be a job for two.

If you have mastered four legs for a chair, a table will seem easy by comparison. Where the ground is uneven or there are small children involved, four legs are undoubtedly the answer. Rectangles are more usual than square tables, and seat more people. As suggested before, a pair of matching tables is a viable solution to

Figure 15 A slatted-top table with tusk tenon construction.

the problem of size. Not only will you be dealing with two smaller pieces of work, but you will spread some of the cost, be able to use your timber more economically, and even save on the size of clamps needed!

All of the above advice also applies to occasional tables, but with these you can afford to be more whimsical and inventive. Picnic tables (those ubiquitous and unstable devices with fixed bench-type seating) are to be avoided in domestic settings as they rarely complement the grounds or the house. I have encountered many of these which display an unnerving propensity for tipping over if the weight on each side is not balanced, rather like a set of scales – one person leaving the table can cause havoc! Folding tables, always useful, are really meant to be of a limited size and weight, so that one person can erect, carry and store them. Lightweight painted

softwood is often used in commercial designs, and inevitably has a limited life prolonged only by winter storage and regular repainting, which nonetheless does nothing to diminish their popularity.

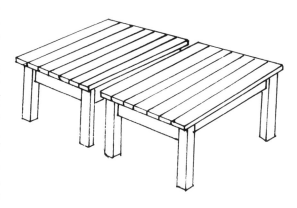

Figure 16 A pair of matching tables.

Figure 17 A folding table.

Figure 18 A rustic pergola shades a path.

PLANT SUPPORTS

Pergolas

Pergolas have been with us from Roman times and are meant to provide shade. Although this is useful in Britain it is not as necessary (sadly) as it is in the Mediterranean. Often they are an excuse to display climbing plants, certainly the only practical reason I had for my own. They are very useful, however, if they can accommodate seating and a table to provide a

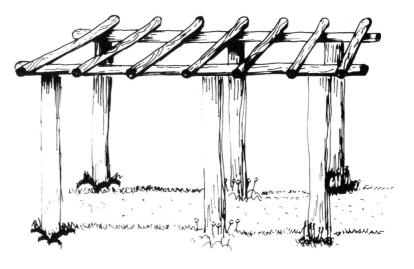

shady lunching place. Failing this they should always offer a focal point, or connect one part of the garden with another. They usually have a flat roof, making them easy to construct, which is supported by posts of various kinds. Mine, in fact has a sloping roof, higher on the side connected to the house in order to clear a window frame, and lower on the free-standing side to bring the flowers within view. Bringing a vertical dimension into the garden is important as it encourages you to view all of the garden as you raise your eyes, making it seem larger. A single pair of posts with a crosspiece will fit into most gardens, and provide excellent colour over a gateway.

Figure 19 A rustic rose arch (above).

Figure 20 Trellis with laths arranged laterally (above right).

Trellis-Work

Trellis screens can have a pattern of squares or diamonds, depending on whether the laths are used diagonally or at right angles to the frame. They can be bought ready made in a variety of shapes and sizes, but as with everything else often not the shape or size that is needed. Their construction is simple and quick using the right tools, and if suitable section timber is used, small buildings can be erected using little else.

Planters, Window Boxes and Troughs

The wooden planters discussed here are square; half barrels and other circular shapes being beyond the scope of this book.

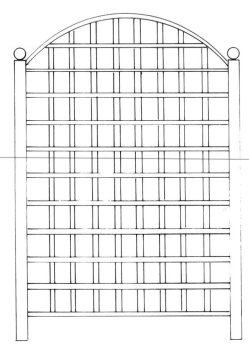

Figure 21 Trellis with laths arranged at right angles.

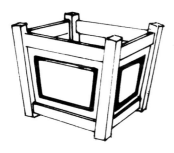

Figure 22 Wooden planter with splayed sides and fielded panels.

Window boxes and troughs, on the other hand, are trough shaped, that is rectangular, and differ only in size. Home-made window boxes are the best, because they will fit your windowsills perfectly rather than not quite fitting anyone's. To place such a box on a sloping sill, place a pair of wedges underneath the full width of the box. Wall brackets may support a box under a window with no sill. A restraining wire running around the top of the box and attached to the wall on both sides is recommended in both cases.

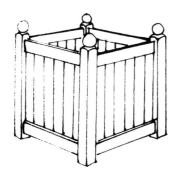

Figure 23 'Versailles' planter with tongue and grooved panels.

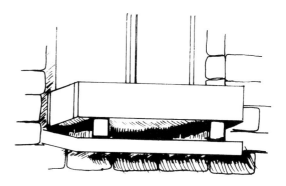

Figure 24 Compensate for sloping sills with full-width wedges to support the window box.

This may seem limiting at first, but there are a number of ways to produce different effects and this is true of all furniture. Here are a few suggestions:

- Construction: panels, boards, external corner posts and size
- Integral decoration: bevels, mouldings, finials, feet
- Applied decoration: preservative, paint (colour, stencil, sponged), varnish

Figure 25 Decorative wall brackets support a windowbox where there is no sill.

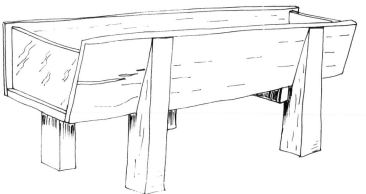

Figure 26 A large sturdy trough in a native hardwood provides a generous planting area.

Figure 27 A small arbour with one entrance provides a focal point and plant support (below).

Troughs are a good alternative to a small flower bed. They are big enough to retain moisture, but are also difficult to move when planted, so site them carefully.

SMALL STRUCTURES

Arbours

An arbour is an open roofed and sided structure. Originally they were temporary supports, but became popular for displaying climbing roses as the new varieties were bred. Although they are often made from wire and as such can be bought in kit form, there is really very little to them and could easily be made with a basic frame and trellis screens. Their roofs are traditionally domed or pitched, the later being more easily made. They may be very small, just large enough to walk through, or made spacious enough to accommodate a seat.

Summer Houses

Summer houses are not necessarily fully weatherproof, but offer more protection than an arbour. They will have a clad roof and at least one solid wall against which there is usually a seat. In this form they are sometimes known as pavilions. If made with rustic poles, ideally sweet chestnut, they are well within the scope of the beginner.

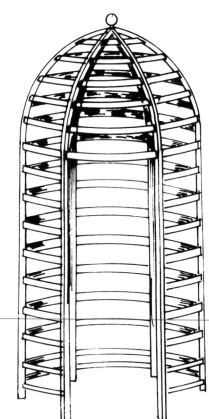

HARD LANDSCAPING

Decking

Decking is not only a stylistic device used to impart a minimalist or modern atmosphere to an urban garden, although it is

Figure 28 A rustic summer house.

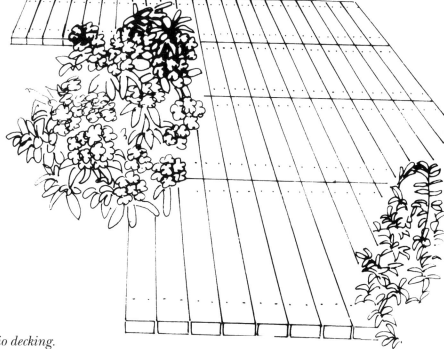

Figure 29 Patio decking.

admirably suited for this use. For roof gardens or terraces, it can be used to provide a secondary surface on which to place heavy objects, such as furniture or containers. It can also be used to create a continuous level surface over uneven ground, or alternatively provide a change of level, such as extra wide steps.

Bridges

All you essentially need to span a small body of water is a plank. However, you may wish to elaborate on this reflecting the nature of your pond and garden. A wildlife pond with planted edges may not need a dramatic structure which draws the eye away from the main point of interest. A formal, hard-edged pond will need a bridge which looks more urban than rural. The type of timber chosen and the colours used will produce these effects just as well and rather less arduously than attempting to build a suspension bridge in the garden. The simplest bridges are flat, simply planked across their width on sturdy bearers. Handrails may continue a decorative theme, as well as being a safety feature.

Gates

A garden's entrance may suggest welcome, or prohibition and secrecy, grandeur or modesty, rurality or urban sophistication.

Figure 30 A Japanese-style bridge with handrail.

Figure 31 A rectangular pond or stream is spanned with a simple flat bridge.

Figure 32 This gate would complement Edwardian or Victorian architecture.

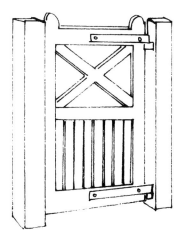

Figure 33 This gate would suit a variety of architectural styles.

Figure 34 This style of construction is best suited to a rural environment.

It is therefore an important interface between your private world and that outside for everyone who enters it. Not only are garden gates which portray character difficult to buy ready made, they are also expensive considering the materials they actually use. Any family with young children or dogs requires the security of a gate which is tailor made for the opening, this inevitably increases the cost unless you are prepared to make one yourself. This important first indication of the nature of your private world is well worth taking some time over – I saw one into which was cut a hole the exact size and shape of the head of the resident dog, including the ears. No-one entering was in any doubt as to the character of those within .

Timber

UNDERSTANDING TIMBER

Wood is a natural material, and so subject to a huge number of variables; no two pieces are the same. Understanding these factors is either boring or fascinating according to your inclination, but knowing the properties of a piece of wood enables us to predict its likely behaviour, and to

build out potential problems which could result in our lovingly made bench (or whatever) falling apart after its first winter.

A humble bench will have to endure freezing cold, wet winters and baking hot summers, and these extremes of temperature and humidity will cause the wood to shrink and swell in turn. The effects of exposure to the elements will exaggerate any tendency to warp, twist, or split, so it is

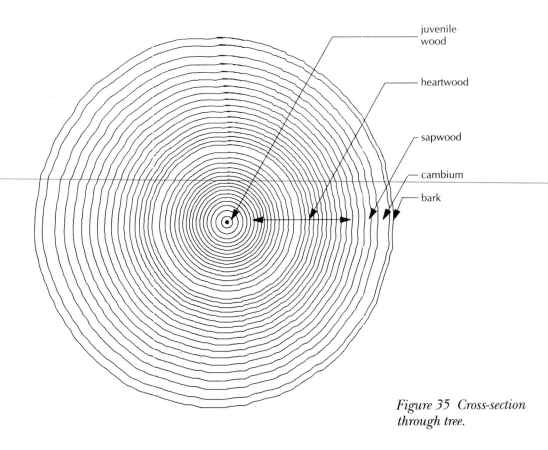

Figure 35 Cross-section through tree.

even more important that these factors are allowed for when making garden furniture than in the case of, say, a sideboard or a coffee table.

We are all familiar with the pattern of growth rings seen when a tree is sliced across its trunk. As children we counted the rings to determine the age of the tree, and may have noticed especially thick or thin rings, denoting a wet or dry year. These rings are made up of cells which form fibres running along the length of the tree, and which for our purposes may best be visualised as a bundle of drinking straws. The tree's intention in producing these bundles is not to provide us with a useful material, but to hold itself up, store food and transport water to the leaves and fruit, where the serious matters of photosynthesis and reproduction take place. Figure 35 shows how these functions are achieved by different parts of the trunk; from the centre outwards we see: juvenile wood (the fast growing, sapling stage of a tree's life), heartwood (this is the supporting part of the tree), sapwood (the food storage and water conduit), cambium (the cell-producing department) and lastly the bark.

Of these, as users of the timber for structural purposes we can see that the heartwood is the useful part; what's good enough for the tree is good enough for us. The sapwood is often hard to distinguish from the heartwood, and indeed in many cases is often used along with it, but it should be noted that even in the case of a hard, durable timber such as oak it will be softer and more prone to insect attack. Cambium and bark have no structural properties, and are likely to appear on a piece of work only as a decorative element in a rustic design. In most species the bark will fall off of its own accord as the timber dries, and there is a case for removing what is both a moisture trap and a nice environment for insects.

I have left the juvenile wood till last as its

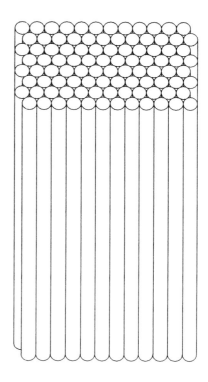

Figure 36 Wood fibres.

inclusion has caused the downfall of many a piece of work. As its name implies, this dates from the first years of the tree's life, and has three inherent problems for the user. Firstly, the rings are relatively widely spaced which means that the wood is softer. A general rule is that, all other things being equal, the closer the rings the harder the timber. Secondly the curvature of the rings is very tight, and as will be explained later the rings of a tree's growth try to straighten themselves out with time. Thirdly, radial splits in timber start at the centre of the tree. Figure 37 shows a cross-section of a piece of timber with included juvenile wood – exhibiting typical distortions.

Almost all problems with stability of timber – that is, its ability to retain a shape –

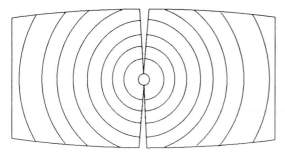

Figure 37 Juvenile wood.

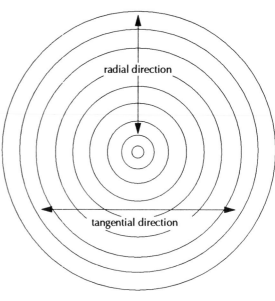

Figure 38 Radial and tangential.

are associated with shrinkage. This cannot be prevented, as wood shrinks both on initial drying and on subsequent reductions in humidity, but it can be allowed for in the eventual construction in which it is used – provided that the shrinkage is fairly consistent. As with the simple exclusion of juvenile wood, there are strategies which may be employed at the stage of conversion (where the tree or 'butt' is sawn into planks) which can make a good deal of difference. Very few of us will be carrying out this process, but a quick look at the end grain (as with the slice through a tree, the exposed ends of the 'drinking straws') can tell us whether the plank is likely to behave itself, and therefore whether we ought to take it home or leave it in the timber merchant's yard!

Shrinkage in timber is greater in the tangential than in the radial direction. Where the plank is cut radially, known as 'quarter sawn', the tangential section is small and consistent across the width of the plank. This results in a very stable piece of timber, in which shrinkage is min-

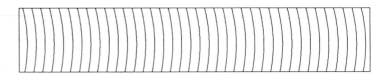

Figure 39 Radial (quarter) sawn timber.

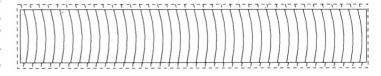

Figure 40 Radial (quarter) sawn timber showing shrinkage pattern.

imized and, just as important, consistent. Where the plank is cut at right angles to the radial direction, known as 'block' or 'flat sawn', the tangential section is very large. This maximizes shrinkage, and also

Figure 41 Tangential (flat) sawn timber.

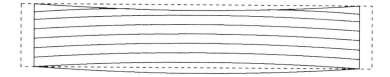

Figure 42 Tangential (flat) sawn timber showing effects of shrinkage.

encourages the plank to 'cup' as the outer rings shrink at a greater rate than the inner. Where a plank is neither quarter nor perfectly flat sawn, the tensions which develop as shrinkage occurs are uneven and will result in pronounced distortion – the end grain of such planks shows the tree's rings as strong diagonal lines. Figure 43 shows how planks cut in these various ways from a butt will behave on drying.

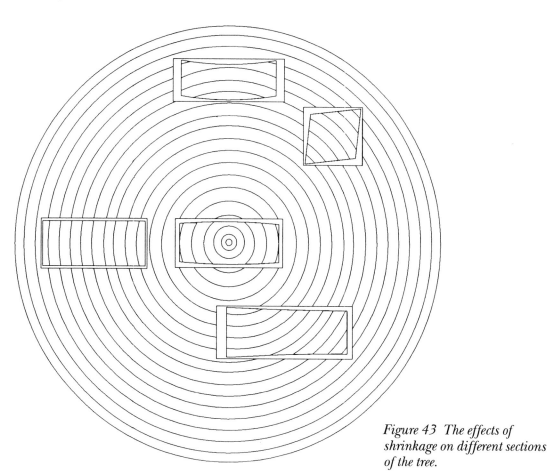

Figure 43 The effects of shrinkage on different sections of the tree.

If nature were not involved, all trees would be straight, with evenly spaced rings, no branches and no damage. As it is, trees assume all kinds of shapes according to their environment and experience. Some will merely bend, others grow in a twisting spiral. A nasty accident can result in a split stem, the tree throwing out two leaders from a break, and even different soil conditions result in erratic growth patterns. These distortions continue to affect the timber long after it is felled: a bend or spiral will tend to straighten, causing a twist or a bow to develop in an initially straight piece of wood. Careful consideration of the growth pattern of the tree from which the timber was cut, together with an understanding of how the plank was cut, are necessary if your furniture is to be the same shape in a couple of years as when it was made.

TIMBER SPECIES

Timber falls neatly into two categories: hardwoods and softwoods. This sounds simple, but in reality there are hardwoods that are softer than most softwoods, and vice versa. What the classification really alludes to is the distinction between deciduous and coniferous trees; those with broad leaves and those with needle-shaped leaves. Thus yew (which yields a timber which is extremely hard), is technically a softwood, whilst balsa is a hardwood. In many ways it is more meaningful to categorize timber as native or imported, since this has more to do with where and in what form it may be purchased. In recent years native timber has become more and more attractive due to the increase in price of imported woods. As a result, English oak is now often cheaper than that from America, although this is subject to continual currency fluctuations.

Both hardwoods and softwoods are used for garden furniture, and so the choice comes down to individual characteristics. The most important of these for the garden furniture maker are strength and rot-resistance, followed by relative ease of working, availability and price. It is very nearly possible to have your cake and eat it here, as some very workable, rot-resistant timbers are not expensive, although you won't find any of these in a DIY superstore or even a typical timber merchant's yard. What you will find in your local DIY superstore is pre-packaged 'pine' of indeterminate species. Generally this is hemlock or some other quick-growing timber, and may not be examined due to its packaging. This is not the drawback it might at first appear, since without exception this is unsuitable for our purpose, being soft, unstable and expensive.

It is never a bad idea to look at the timbers used by others in furniture of the style we wish to build, and if it is a few years old then so much the better, as we may then assess its durability. To many, garden furniture of quality means teak, hence its inclusion in this list, although nowadays it is too

Figure 44 Coniferous (left) *and deciduous* (right) *leaves.*

A mixture of native timbers in a fencing yard.

endangered and expensive to consider for this purpose.

Imported 'Red' Hardwoods

Danta (*Nesogordonia papaverifera*)
An African hardwood, strong, durable and fairly stable. Has a high resistance to abrasion, and it has been used in shipbuilding. It is moderately hard to work, and has some blunting effect on tools.

Iroko (*Chlorophora excelsa/regia*)
An African hardwood, almost as strong as teak, also very durable and stable. As an exterior timber its resistance to rot is useful, and it has been used in place of teak for various purposes. It is hard to work,

and has some blunting effect on tools. It is prone to splintering, and some find the dust a severe irritant.

African Mahogany (*Khaya ivorensis/ anthotheca/grandifoliola*)
This group of timbers is marketed as one, and its members share many characteristics. They are moderately strong and very stable. As an exterior timber they are durable, and are used in shipbuilding. Average in workability and tool blunting, a good all-round hardwood.

Makoré (*Tieghemella heckelii*)
This African hardwood is strong, durable and stable. Again it is used in shipbuilding, and also exterior joinery. It is very hard to

work, and has a severe blunting effect on tools. It also has a very irritant dust.

Teak (*Tectona grandis*)

This hardwood is strong, durable and stable. As an exterior timber its resistance to rot is well known and it has been extensively used in shipbuilding. It is hard to work, and has a severe blunting effect on tools. It is a very expensive timber and in the main originates from rainforest areas, although some managed, sustainable plantations are operating.

Utile (*Entandrophragma utile*)

An African hardwood, strong, durable and fairly stable. It is quite easy to work, and has a moderate blunting effect on tools. It is a readily available timber, suitable for exterior work.

Native, European and North American Hardwoods

Ash – European (*Fraxinus excelsior*) – American (*Fraxinus americana*)

This hardwood is very strong and quite stable. It is fairly easy to work, with a moderate blunting effect on tools. Much used for chair-making, and also coachbuilding. A tough and (if native) relatively inexpensive timber, with a bold figure.

Beech – European (*Fagus sylvatica*)

This hardwood is very strong but neither durable nor stable. It is fairly easy to work, with a moderate blunting effect on tools. Much used as a general hardwood in the UK, although requiring extensive preservative treatment for exterior use.

Sweet Chestnut (*Castanea sativa*)

This hardwood is moderate in strength, unusually durable and very stable. It is easy to work, with little blunting effect on tools. Used as a substitute for oak (which it resembles) and for fencing, due to its high resistance to rot. An inexpensive native hardwood with a bold figure.

Elm – English/Dutch (*Ulmus procera*)

This hardwood is neither strong, durable or stable. It is average in workability, depending on the example, with some blunting effect on tools. Uses include coffin-making, boatbuilding and some agricultural uses. Can be a very attractive timber, with a very bold figure.

Elm – Rock (*Ulmus thomasii*)

This Canadian elm is very strong and quite durable, although not very stable. It is moderately hard to work, with some blunting effect on tools. Often used in boatbuilding.

Elm – White/American (*Ulmus americana*)

As rock elm, but not quite as strong and more workable.

Elm – Wych (*Ulmus glabra*)

This native elm is much stronger, slightly more stable, and no more durable than *procera*. It is average in workability, with some blunting effect on tools. Uses include coffin-making and boatbuilding. Preferable for exterior work.

Oak – American Red (*Quercus rubra*)

This oak is quite strong, fairly durable and fairly stable. It is reasonably workable, with some blunting effect on tools. Not as suitable for exterior work as other oaks, but has an attractive reddish colour.

Oak – American White (*Quercus alba/ prinus/lyrata*)

This oak is strong, durable and fairly stable. It is reasonably workable, with some blunting effect on tools. Good, straight-grained exterior timber.

Oak – European (*Quercus robur/petraea*)

This oak is very strong, durable and fairly stable. It is workable, with some blunting effect on tools. This timber has been used for almost every purpose for centuries, from housebuilding and shipbuilding to fences and gates. Suitable for exterior work and available for such in lower grades at reasonable cost.

Softwoods

Identification of softwoods is quite difficult, partly because there are so many similar looking timbers within each family, and partly because the timber trade seems to retail every softwood as 'pine'. The situation is further obscured by the casual use of more than one name for a single species – Douglas fir, for example, is also referred to as 'BC' or British Columbian pine – or by giving one name to a number of species. Therefore this section is restricted to a small group of softwoods which are especially suitable for use in garden furniture, and which are available under, at most, two names.

Cedar (*Cedrus spp.*)
A durable, moderately strong and very stable softwood. It is easy to work, and has a distinctive scent. Cedar is used for the more expensive greenhouses, and is suitable for garden furniture.

Douglas Fir/British Columbian Pine (*Pseudotsuga menziesii*)
A strong, durable and stable softwood. It works well, although it can be brittle, and is usually almost knot free. Easy to obtain, it is well worth the higher price than is asked for Scots pine, especially for exterior work.

Pitch Pine/Longleaf Pine (*Pinus palustris*)
A heavy, resinous softwood, very durable and with a strength approaching that of oak. Workability is good where the high resin content does not make it sticky, and it is usually knot free. Very suitable for exterior work, although heavy.

Scots Pine/Baltic Redwood (*Pinus sylvestris*)
The most likely timber to be found labelled merely 'pine'. If selected for quality, and relatively free of knots, its strength is around 60 per cent, and stiffness 50 per cent, of English oak. It works easily, although pockets of resin may cause problems, and is quite stable. Its durability is not high and thorough preservative treatment is required when used for exterior work.

Seeing the Wood for the Trees

If the foregoing list of timbers seems bewildering, do not worry. The chances are that many of them will not be easily available to you and the cost of some will render them inappropriate for much garden furniture. Choose according to the job in hand; durability is important, for example, but does the table you are making really need to last for a hundred years, or would twenty-five be enough? If making a rustic bench, then an imported 'red' hardwood will look quite wrong, better to use a lower and less expensive grade of native timber such as oak or sweet chestnut. If a piece is to be painted, then a good softwood such as Douglas fir is more than adequate, and Scots pine will do very well if looked after.

The likelihood is that you will settle on two or three favourites which are available without too much trouble, and tailor your projects accordingly.

FINDING AND BUYING TIMBER

Recycling

Perhaps this heading should be: Finding *or* buying timber. As a society we consume a vast quantity of all kinds of timber and inevitably end up throwing quite a lot away. In most cases timber, once finished with, is not in a fit state for reuse, but that still leaves a lot that can be recycled. There is a certain etiquette to poking around in other people's skips, but properly handled a large number of pine framed and panelled doors may be amassed, yielding some useful sizes of material. Some very ugly furniture was made from solid oak and other timbers between the wars, and to most people is worth very little – yet a single wardrobe of this type will make a table, at least. On a more prosaic level, pallets are often to be had for nothing or next to nothing, and soon become very stylish decking for a patio. Once you are aware of the possibilities, all kinds of old sheds, fence posts and so on will appear before your eyes. One advantage of using such timber is that it is generally well seasoned and ready planed.

Those who live in the countryside should develop an instinct for a thicket clearing and the sound of a chainsaw in the distance should set the ears pricking. More than one woodworker I know travels with a bowsaw in the boot of the car, and one even carries a chainsaw, although this is extreme and may frighten strangers! Once you become known as a timber scavenger, people will start to offer you all sorts of useful (and not so useful) stuff. Accept it all – you can always have a bonfire, but there is a special satisfaction in producing a piece of furniture that cost nothing (except the time) to make.

Specialist Timber Merchants

It seems likely, though, that some wood will need to be bought. How difficult a matter this will be depends firstly on where you are and secondly on which species you are looking for. The timber trade is one of the older branches of commerce and many specialist firms have been trading since the eighteenth or nineteenth century, often from the same site. This means that they are located around the long-established commercial ports and industrial towns, river and canal links being the only way to transport imported timber in those days, much as businesses cluster around motorway links now.

These are often the most knowledgeable suppliers and they should carry stock of a wide variety of imported timbers, certainly most of the species listed earlier in this chapter, but they can be difficult to deal with. It is not unknown for a customer to be turned away simply because there is no company procedure for handling a cash sale. If you are not within striking distance of one of these, all is not lost as they will arrange delivery of fairly small quantities if you are prepared to wait.

Thankfully, one or two such suppliers have turned their attention to the growing market in small quantities of timber for amateur users and should be forthcoming with both advice and prompt delivery. It is easy to distinguish between the former, who probably do not advertise at all, and the latter, who advertise extensively in woodworking magazines. If you are asked for your company name when making a telephone enquiry, the chances are that the firm is not geared to the small customer (a very long-established timber merchant once defined a 'small customer' to me as being one who is buying less than fifty cubic feet of timber…).

Local Sawmills

Countryside-dwellers are well served by comparison, as they should find that there is a fairly local sawmill who will deal in mainly native timbers, although many of these now carry some stock of the more popular imported hardwoods. These sawmills will be used to dealing with small orders and the best of them will allow the visitor to root around the yard and select their own boards. This is quite a good strategy, as I always see something that I had not known that I wanted, and on average take away twice as much timber as planned. This kind of supplier will often have short boards and odd bits at reduced prices and it is worth building up a relationship. While on the subject of rural suppliers, thinking laterally can pay dividends. Fencing contractors can be a useful source of timber 'in the round', that is unplanked and often still wearing its bark, and even sawn native timber, particularly sweet chestnut.

Builder's Merchants

If your project requires pressure treated timber (see Chapter 9 on preservation), or if there is no other convenient supplier, then you will be shopping at a builder's merchant. Some carry more timber than others – if all you see are bricks or baths then try elsewhere. The type that we are interested in will have stacks of sawn four-by-two in the yard, and hopefully racks of planed softwood (PAR; 'planed all round') under cover, along with skirting board and architrave mouldings. The level of advice or even courtesy in these places ranges, in my experience, from one extreme to the other, but since they also keep coach bolts, brackets, hinges and many other useful things it is worth finding a good one. Many an elegant pergola or arbor has started out as an unpromising collection of sawn, tanalized four-by-two next to a pile of sand.

Planed softwood from this kind of outlet is most often Scots pine (see above), and its quality will vary greatly. You should be allowed to select from the stock in the racks, and in this way surprisingly good timber can be obtained. Two warnings: one, do not be tempted to buy sawn softwood here to plane up yourself, as the quality and species will be quite different, generally rather poor hemlock; and two, do not buy hardwoods here, as the price can be up to three times what you will pay at a sawmill.

PROCESSING THE RAW MATERIAL

As Supplied

There is another consideration to be made when choosing one of these different sources of timber, or indeed when choosing which type, and that is the extent to which the timber has been processed ready for use.

Just as a fish may be purchased at various stages of processing, from a complete fish straight from the boat, to a filleted example from a fishmonger, and ultimately a fish finger, so timber is supplied in different states by different suppliers. The 'straight from the boat' equivalent is timber 'in the round', that is, a log or butt which has not been sawn into boards. In practice, timber will only be purchased like this in small diameters for rustic work, and from a fencing contractor or similar. The first stage of

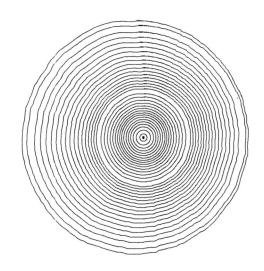

Figure 45 Timber 'in the round'.

Timber 'in the round'.

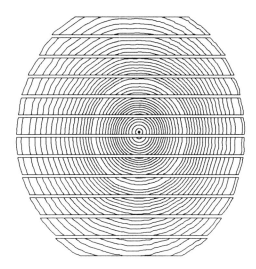

Figure 46 Timber 'waney edged' (above).

Figure 47 Timber 'square edged'.

conversion (filleting!) occurs when the butt is sawn into boards, or 'planked'. This is the state in which most native hardwoods are supplied, sliced from the butt with the edges left untrimmed; described as 'waney edged'. Stage three consists of trimming the board, removing the bark and uneven edges to give a straight, square plank. This is referred to as 'S/E' (square edged) or 'SSE' (sawn square edged) timber. Imported timbers are supplied in this state, as straight-edged timber may be packed closer for shipping, with little wasted space. For most suppliers of commercial timber this is as far as the conversion process goes, the customer carrying out any planing to size and so on. Having said this, Scots pine may be bought PAR (planed all round), although not in the better qualities, and some suppliers of other timbers will carry out planing to order, although at extra cost.

Waney-edged boards of English oak.

TIMBER

Halved timber.

Further Processing

This means that any additional processing of the timber must be done by, or at least arranged by, the end user. How much of a problem this represents depends on the answers to the following questions:

1. In what state may the chosen timber be purchased?
2. How much further processing will be required for use?
3. Do I have the facilities for this further processing?
4. If not, can this processing be arranged?

Let us look at the most extreme example possible, and imagine that we have pur-

chased a newly felled tree of, say, oak, and wish to use the timber planed all round. The stages involved, and the equipment required, are as follows.

Trimming the Butt

This is the process of removing branches to give a clean butt. It may be done with a bowsaw if the branches are small in diameter, or a chainsaw. This is a process which can easily be undertaken by the end user, although some help will be needed turning the butt to reach all the way round it. Depending on the size of the butt, this may call for some friends with levers, or a tractor. The hazards at this stage extend beyond mere lacerations – stay clear!

Planking

Although theoretically this can be (and was historically) done by hand, in reality a machine is needed. This may be a chain-saw mill (a frame which guides a chainsaw safely along the butt) which is just conceivably within the scope of a keen amateur, or better a mobile band mill. This is a portable horizontal bandsaw which is taken to the tree. These are wonderful things that first caught on after the 1987 hurricane, and there are quite a lot of them now being operated by one-man businesses all over the country.

Squaring the Edges

Well within the scope of the garden furniture maker, this may be done by hand saw slowly, with a hand-held circular saw carefully, or with a table saw (a static circular-saw bench) quickly and accurately. Alternatively the man with the band mill will probably undertake this process.

Seasoning

Depending on the eventual use of the timber, this is simply a matter of stacking the boards (with sticks in between to ensure an even flow of air) and waiting a year or so.

Planing all Round

Fanatics may relish the prospect of hand planing acres of timber, but if there is any quantity to be done it is best left to a planer-thicknesser. This is a static machine which is owned by many serious amateur woodworkers (*see* Chapter 4 on tools and equipment), but various businesses from the local joiner to the sawmill will carry this out by arrangement.

Choosing Timber for the Job

It will be seen from the foregoing that any amount of post-purchase processing is possible. Buying and processing a tree is a pursuit in itself, so the example given is very extreme – the most one will ever really have to do is to square the edges and plane all round.

It will also be seen that choosing an appropriate timber and supplier for the style of work in hand will save a lot of work and frustration, the more so if the style of work is chosen to suit the facilities available. For example, a semi-rustic bench made from waney edged oak can be achieved without any processing at all, as may a Lutyens bench constructed from PAR Scots pine.

Anything is possible, but not everything is probable!

TOOLS

CHOOSING AND USING TOOLS

According to some it is our ability to use tools that sets us apart from other animals. Perhaps this explains our compulsion to refine them into ever more specialized sub-divisions, proliferating the number of tools available to a bewildering extent. An eighteenth-century carpenter making the kind of things discussed in this book would have felt well equipped if he owned perhaps twenty or thirty tools. It was also absolutely necessary that he could carry them all in a bag over his shoulder. How do we reconcile this with the thousands of woodworking tools now available? Well the same carpenter probably owned only one pair of trousers, so it could be down to our increase in general sophistication. We also expect things to happen very quickly, of course, and electricity has made hard manual work seem needless. I suspect that at least part of the explanation is that tools are simply attractive things to own, and if one tool is good, then two tools must be twice as good!

The point of all this is that it is not essential to have a vast amount of equipment. The type of work discussed in this book can be done with a small number of basic tools. In the following chapter, these basics are marked thus: *essential*. In the same way as a journey may be made more easily in a car than on a bicycle, there are some tools and pieces of equipment which will make life easier and allow more ambitious projects to be undertaken; these items are marked: *useful*. The next logical step is, I suppose, a helicopter. Tools

and machines in this class are really intended for the professional user, and for the amateur must be regarded as overkill. Nonetheless some are included in the interests of covering the subject fully, and will at least make the reader aware of the possibilities – not least of finding someone with such a piece of equipment to help with an unusual project. Where marked at all, these will be identified as: *luxury*. At the end of this chapter a couple of tool kits are suggested, based on these identifications.

Hand and Power

Tools powered by hand and those powered by electric motors are dealt with together according to the function which they perform. This is a more meaningful system of categorization these days, when a 'hand router' more often means an electrically powered router which is held in the hand rather than a tool which is powered by the muscle of the user. Improving technology means that cordless, or battery powered, tools are further blurring the distinction.

Safety

Any tool, whether hand or electrically powered, which is capable of altering the shape of a piece of wood can do the same to a person. Working with such tools carries an element of risk, and it is the responsibility of the user to be aware of it, and to minimize it as far as possible. When working, especially with power tools, do not wear loose clothes or jewellery, ensure that the work is securely held, and wear eye protection and ear defenders. Keep your working area free from obstructions, and of children and animals. A dust mask or respirator (these are discussed later) should be worn whenever dust is present in the atmosphere and not just while the cut is being made. The noise of a power tool acts as a warning that danger is present and can lead to complacency when using silent hand tools, but these are also dangerous.

Try to develop a safe 'attitude'. Get into the habit of thinking through an operation before carrying it out, check that all is as it should be before starting and remain alert while the operation is underway. When using potentially dangerous equipment, remember that safety is your responsibility, both for yourself and for others.

THE TOOLS OF THE TRADE

(**NB** Tools are traditionally offered in imperial sizes and this convention is observed here.)

SAWS AND SAWING

This is a core operation, and it is hard to imagine making anything from wood without some kind of saw. The hand-powered variety fall into three categories: handsaws, meaning a large flat blade with a handle at one end, back saws, which are shorter (10–14in) than a handsaw, with a brass or steel 'back' along the top edge of the blade, and frame saws, which have a narrower blade in tension, held at each end by the leg of a frame which may also be the handle.

Handsaws

Traditional handsaws are graded according to their length, in inches, and the number of teeth per inch (TPI) on the blade. These two measurements indicate

the suitability of the saw for a particular type of work, as follows:

24–26in 3–6 TPI	a rip saw, for cutting along the grain – little used now
22–26 in 6–8 TPI	a cross-cut saw, for cutting across the grain – *useful*
20–22 inch 10–12 TPI	a panel saw, for cutting thin panels both with and across the grain – *useful*

All of these saws may be resharpened, by the skilled user or a specialist. This cannot be said of a relatively new type of handsaw, the 'hardpoint' type. These saws are reasonably priced, generally with plastic handles, and have hardened teeth. While this means that they cannot be sharpened and are therefore disposable, they are ferociously sharp and hold their edge well. While old hands may find them too light and flexible, their ease of use is impressive – *essential*.

Back Saws

These are shorter versions of handsaws, designed for the very accurate cutting of joints and accurate cross-cutting of smaller section timber. The blade is stiffened by a 'back' – a heavier piece of brass or steel folded over the top edge of the blade. This also adds weight, enabling the cut to be made without 'pushing' the blade, giving greater control. The most common type is the tenon saw, between 10 and 14in in length, and having 10–14 TPI – *useful*. Again these are available as 'hardpoint', although this is less of an advantage with a tenon saw.

Frame Saws

A frame saw works by holding a replaceable blade in tension between two arms of a frame. The advantage of this is that a narrow blade will remain straight in use, which is useful for cutting curves and is also less likely to 'bind' or stick in that cut. Of the many types available, only two are relevant to the making of garden furniture; the bowsaw and the coping saw.

The bowsaw is derived from a traditional European tool with a wooden frame tensioned by means of a winding stick and twine, but is more like a metal cutting hacksaw in construction. The ribbon-sized blade is of hardened steel with deep-gulleted teeth, which makes for a fast cut in wet or dry material. It is held in tension by a cam-lever on a tubular steel frame. These saws are cheap, indestructible and perfect for fast cutting, especially of green (freshly cut) timber – *essential*.

The coping saw is a small, fine-frame saw with a very narrow blade. The blade may be swivelled in the frame, making tight curves and changes of direction possible. Used for curved work and joint cutting – *useful*.

While on the subject of frame saws, a quick word about hacksaws. These are metal cutting versions of the bowsaw, and quite simply everybody should have one. They will get you out of all sorts of trouble – *essential*.

Power Saws

These may be sub-divided into: hand-held, and static. Chainsaws are not discussed due to the very high incidence of accidents with these tools and the fact that a little knowledge is a dangerous thing. If you wish to use a chainsaw, then seek professional tuition in their safe operation. The remaining relevant hand-held power saws are circular saws and jigsaws; the first giving straight cuts, and the second being capable of both straight and shaped work. Static machines worth considering are: bandsaws, which make straight or curved cuts with or across the grain; saw benches, which have an inverted circular saw permanently mounted in a table, and are good for straight cuts mostly with the grain, and radial-arm saws, an overhead mounted circular saw used mostly for accurate cross-cutting.

Hand-held Circular Saws

Essentially a rotary blade mounted on the end of a motor, these are available with various blade diameters from 6in (giving a depth of cut of 2in) to a fearsome 12in (giving a depth of cut of around 3½in). Useful for rough cross-cutting of boards, they can be persuaded to straighten the edge of a waney-edged board if guided by a straight edge clamped to the board in question. Blades are offered in two forms, high-speed steel (HSS) and tungsten carbide tipped (TCT). Of these, TCT is by far the most useful as it will stay sharper for longer – HSS is only worth considering if all of your work is in softwood. I have tended to use these saws reluctantly, as I find them less than controllable, but have recently started using a cordless version. This is a 5in blade 14.4 volt device, and its smooth running, good balance and lack of a trailing power lead mean that I am using it more and more. It is well worth investigating – *useful*.

Jigsaws

The most versatile of the powered saws, and fairly safe if used properly. They will cut either straight or curved lines and the adept will be able to cut many types of joints with this tool. Disposable blades are offered in a wide variety of tooth sizes and patterns, enabling fast, rough cutting and finer work to be carried out. If you buy only one power tool, it should be a jigsaw – *useful*.

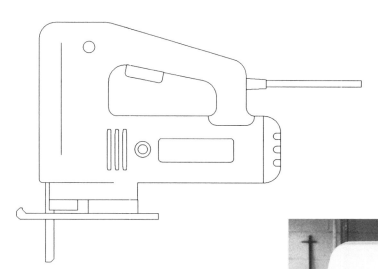

Figure 48 Jigsaw.

Figure 49 Bandsaw.

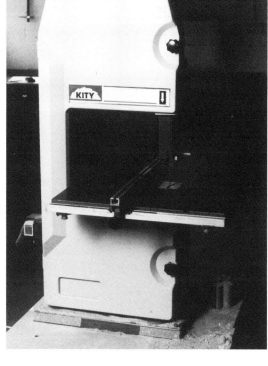

Bandsaws

Like the jigsaw, the bandsaw will perform both straight and curved cuts and is the safest of the static saws to use. The accuracy of these machines allows them to be used for very precise joint cutting – tenons and halved joints are especially suited to being cut on the bandsaw. The blade is a continuous band running on two or three rubber-tyred wheels, and all but the cutting point is enclosed by a case and adjustable guard. As they take up very little space, are quiet in operation and not as costly as some static machines, they are worth considering. The three-wheeled variety are cheaper than those with two, but get through blades rather more quickly – *useful*.

Circular Sawbenches

Like the hand-held variety they are based around a rotary blade (TCT or HSS – *see* above) attached to a motor (either directly or via a belt drive), but in this case securely mounted under a work table with only the part of the blade in use projecting above. An adjustable guard is fitted and with a little instruction most people should feel comfortable using one of these machines. A fence is fixed to the work table to guide the timber through the blade and very accurate cutting is possible. Useful for ripping (cutting along the grain) boards into precise widths. With accessories, accurate

Figure 50 Circular sawbench.

cross-cutting is possible and experienced users can carry out various jointing operations – *luxury*.

Radial-arm saws

These are increasingly finding their way into the garages of amateur woodworkers, hence their inclusion here, but although they are very versatile I have reservations about their safety – I once worked with a man who had severed fingers on two separate occasions, while using one of these saws. Once again we have the rotary sawblade fixed to a motor, this time suspended from a sliding carriage which runs in a movable arm above a work table. These saws are excellent for cross-cutting timber, for which operation the board is placed on the table and the saw pulled across it.

The saw head may be rotated and fixed at any angle in both vertical and lateral planes and the arm itself may be swung around and locked at an angle – also raised and lowered. With all this adjustment a great variety of cuts (including ripping) are possible, although resetting to zero can be

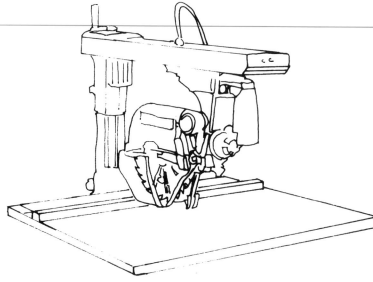

Figure 51 Radial-arm saw.

fiddly. In the hands of a trained, confident operator a radial-arm saw is a powerful production tool, but dangerous for the casual user. If you must have one, then seek professional tuition and proceed carefully.

PLANES AND PLANING

Another core operation. Although it is possible to make wooden objects, even garden furniture, without planing a surface, it would be very limiting to have to. Planing is the process by which a layer is shaved from the surface of the timber. This is done for a number of reasons. Firstly a face or edge can be made perfectly straight and flat in this way, and one surface may be corrected until it is at 90 degrees (or even some other angle) to another. Planing may even be viewed as a surface treatment, leaving a smooth finish, or chamfering an edge.

More important than cosmetic considerations is the requirement to precisely dimension a piece of timber. If we have a piece of wood which measures in section, say, 52mm by 21mm and we want it to be 50mm by 20mm, then only the plane will accomplish this. So the hand plane is used to adjust already cut surfaces and to make them look attractive.

Planing large areas, for example a few boards of sawn timber, is arduous work though, and two types of powered plane are available, hand-held and static.

Hand Planes

The first examples of hand planes were made with wooden bodies (usually beech) with a wide cutting iron held in place with a wooden wedge. The type in use today have cast iron bodies and very controllable adjustment for depth

of cut, the angle at which the cutter sits, and size of mouth. Even more than saws the plane has been refined into a large number of specialist tools, and here we look at the two most relevant to garden furniture making. Also covered here are spokeshaves, which are plane-like tools.

First is the Bailey-pattern bench plane, familiar to most of us, and like saws their specific use and type is defined by their size – albeit translated into a rather obscure numbering system. The most useful sizes out of the eight or nine available are:

04 9¾in by 2in   Smoothing plane – *useful*

05 14in by 2in   Jack plane – *essential*

07 22in by 2⅜in   Jointer plane – *luxury*

The jointer is used for straightening edges (often prior to jointing) where its long sole helps level an uneven surface. The smoother is used for removing imperfections in an already flat surface, and the Jack plane is the 'Jack of all trades', performing all planing tasks fairly well. This is the one to have if one only is bought.

The second really useful hand plane to have is the block plane, so called because its original purpose was to plane the endgrain surface of butcher's blocks. The cutting iron of the block plane is set at a low angle (20 degrees) which helps it to shear-cut the

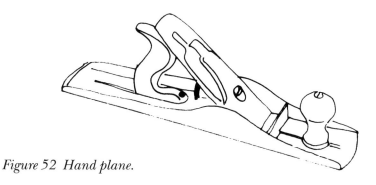

Figure 52 Hand plane.

fibres of end-grain timber. At just over 6in long, this plane fits neatly into the hand and is a good all-round tool – *useful*.

Spokeshaves

The spokeshave is a plane with almost no length to the sole, and is held by two wing type handles, one at each side. Due to its shape, it can follow a curve easily and is much used for shaping and smoothing chair parts and so on. They are available with flat or curved soles and are not expensive – *essential*.

Hand-held Power Planes

These are roughly the same size and shape as bench planes, and are held in the same way. Where the cutter would project through the mouth of a bench plane, the powered variety has a drum, or cutter block, in which two replaceable cutters are fitted. Under power, the block rotates at high speed, providing the cutting action. The front part of the sole is adjustable for depth of cut by twisting the front handle. I confess that I have never had much success with these tools, and view them as a roughing out tool rather than a plane, but others may get on better with them. When planing an edge with a bench plane, it is usual to slip the

fingers of the left hand under the sole to guide it – those who have developed this habit should lose it before using a power plane, or they will lose the tips of their fingers instead. Not a favourite.

Static Planers

These are the other side of the coin to the hand held type, being very accurate indeed, and safe if used correctly. The principle is the same, in that a rotating cutter block does the planing while the wood is passed over it, guided by a split 'sole' in the form of infeed and outfeed tables. The infeed table is adjustable in height for setting the depth of cut, and the large table surface provides effective control. Most planers of this type sold today also have a thicknessing facility. When one face and edge are planed straight and square, the timber is passed under the cutter block on a thicknessing table, fed by powered rollers. This planes the opposite face exactly parallel to the original planed face, resulting in consistently dimensioned timber at speed. If there is any quantity of timber to be planed all round, then this is the only way to do it. To me this is an essential piece of equipment although others will consider it a luxury item, so we will call it *useful* as a compromise.

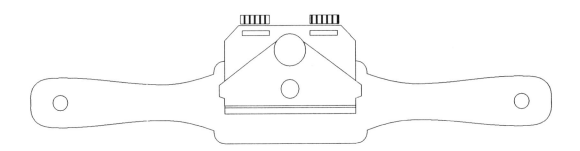

Figure 53 Spokeshave.

Figure 54 Hand-held power plane.

Figure 55 Planer thicknesser.

DRILLS AND DRILLING

Not a glamorous operation, accurate and efficient drilling is nonetheless an important part of the woodworking process. Most people own a power drill, and hand drills hold little mystery, so we will concentrate here mostly on the drill bits themselves. Cordless drills are now very serious pieces of equipment which are capable of heavy work in both timber and masonry and deserve consideration as an alternative to both hand and corded power drills.

Hand Drills

Two forms of hand drills are offered for woodworkers, the brace and the wheel brace. The former is a cranked device used for driving large drill bits slowly, the second is gear

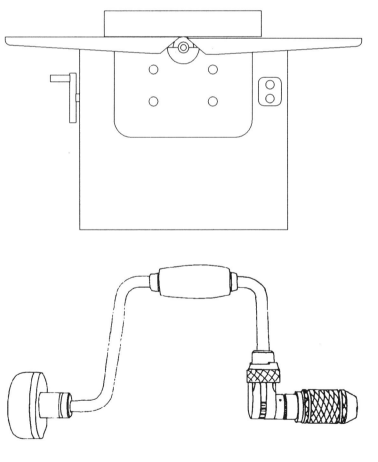

Figure 56 Hand brace.

49

Figure 57
Wheel brace.

driven and is used for smaller drills at higher speed. To a large extent both have been superseded by power and cordless drills, but at least one of these should be in every tool kit – *essential*.

Power Drills

Widely available in many configurations, these are general purpose tools for the woodworker – *useful*. Principle options include: hammer drilling – essential for fixing into masonry; electronic speed control – useful for drilling large diameter holes in timber; and reverse operation – for the easy withdrawal of the drill and for removing screws. All of these are worth having, but it is better to buy a well made drill with few features than a cheap one with all the gadgets, especially if you also have a cordless drill.

Cordless Power Drills

Early examples were fairly weak, but technological improvements have increased the power of these tools to a point where the largest, 14.4 volts with hammer action, can rival mains power drills. They are also offered in 7.2, 9.6 and 12 volts. All offer reverse operation for screw driving and removal, most have variable speed, and many have adjustable torque. The control and balance of the cordless drill means that it will perform many functions traditionally associated with hand drills – *useful*.

Drill Bits

Whichever device is used to supply the rotational force, it is the drill bit which does the cutting. Each of the following types is designed for a specific function and choosing the right one for the job is important.

HSS Twist Drills

The most common form of bit, these are intended for the drilling of metals and often make a poor hole in timber, tending to slip at the start of the cut. Only to be used for wood in the smaller sizes – *useful*.

Lip and Spur Twist Drills

The correct twist drill for timber, these have a small point in the centre to guide the cut, and the cutting edges are ground to give two 'wings', which cut with a planing action – *essential*.

Auger Drills

These have a threaded point in the centre and one or two very deep spiral flutes, ending in cutting edges tipped with spurs. The spurs score the wood allowing the cutting edges to plane away the waste, which is ejected via the spiral flutes. These drills give a clean hole even in large diameters. The older type have a square 'tang', meant to be gripped in the square chuck of a

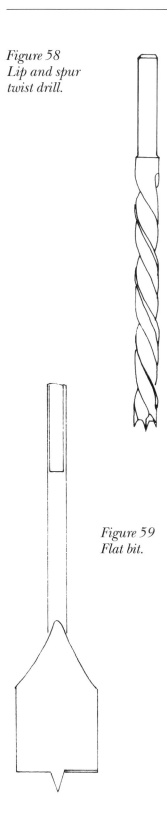

Figure 58
Lip and spur
twist drill.

Figure 59
Flat bit.

cranked brace, while augers designed for modern drills have a round shank ground to produce flats for secure mounting in conventional chucks – *useful*.

Flat Bits

An inexpensive bit for drilling large diameter holes with a mains power drill. As the name suggests, they are flat with a point and spur profile. Although cheap to buy, they are hard to control and can bend easily.

ROUTERS AND ROUTING

Formerly the preserve of the professional, routers are being bought by amateurs at a prodigious rate nowadays and with good reason. A router consists of a high-speed electric motor mounted vertically on a flat base by means of two sliding columns. Thus the router may be moved around on its base, and raised and lowered – known as plunging. On the end of the motor is fitted a special chuck, known as a collet, which will accept cutters with a specific shank size. The smallest routers (between 500 and 900 watts in power) accept cutters with a ¼in shank, midrange machines (between 900 and 1400 watts) will also take cutters with ⅜in shanks, and the most powerful (1600 to over 2000 watts – three horse power!) all sizes including ½in. A new shank size of 8mm is appearing from Europe and will probably replace the two smaller imperial sizes. Most routers are available with electronic speed control.

The advantage of greater power is obvious, but that of the larger shank sizes bears some explanation. A router is a high speed device, and the nature of the cutters is such that they are subject to profound lateral stresses. The smaller the diameter of the shank, the more possibility of it flexing, causing vibration, or even bending which renders it useless. Therefore larger shanks

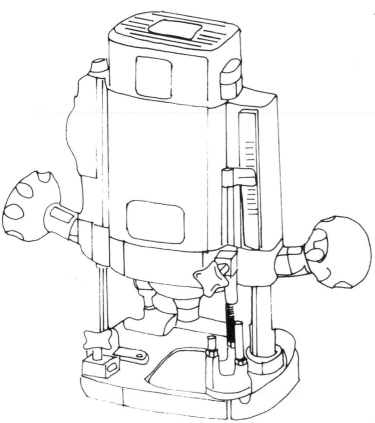

Figure 60 Router.

Figure 61 Router cutters.

are needed for heavy work, although even the smaller routers are great workhorses. Cutters are available in a large range of shapes and sizes, and like circular sawblades are best bought with TCT cutting edges.

It is not within the scope of this book to fully explore the uses of this most versatile of power tools, and the range of accessories available would require a book to themselves. The router is capable of: mortising, tenoning, rebating, grooving, moulding, shaping, jointing and planing, and many other functions – *useful*.

SANDERS AND SANDING

Abrasives are dealt with elsewhere in this book, but the means of applying them are tools. At a simple level this is a sanding block around which the abrasive paper is wrapped. This might be wood, which is easily made, and it may have a cork or felt backing applied to reduce heat created by friction. Figure 62 shows a simple block of this kind. Power tool manufacturers have not ignored this area and electrically powered sanders of various types are available.

Belt Sanders

These have a continuous belt of cloth-backed abrasive, which travels in one direction only leaving straight scratches.

Suitable for rapid stock removal, and 'flattening' uneven areas. In many ways the true powered equivalent of the hand plane – *useful*.

Rotary Sanders

An unsophisticated device which rotates an abrasive disc at high speed, often an accessory for a power drill. These tools are hard to control and leave circular scratches.

Orbital Sanders

Orbital sanders have a square or rectangular pad onto which is fixed (with clips or Velcro) the abrasive. This pad vibrates in a small orbit and leaves a fine finish.

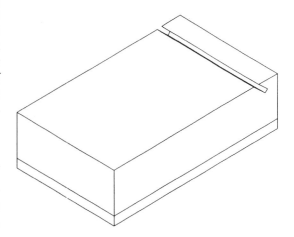

Figure 62 Sanding block.

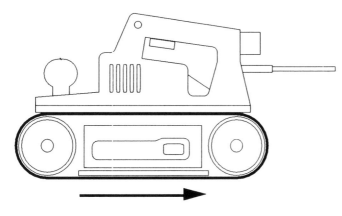

Figure 63 Belt sander.

Random Orbital Sanders

A new development which combines the actions of both the rotary and the orbital sanders, using a round pad to which the abrasive is fixed with Velcro. This action allows for quite rapid stock removal without leaving any discernible scratches, due to the random direction of the abrasive particles. A multi-purpose tool – *useful*.

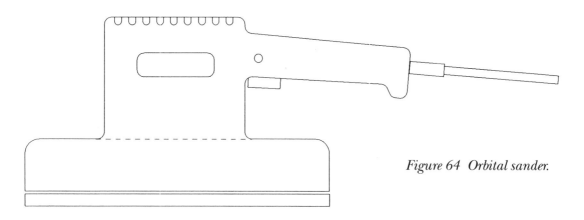

Figure 64 Orbital sander.

Figure 64 Random orbital sander (below).

CHISELS AND CHISELLING

Almost as old as the working of wood, chisels will be found in every tool kit. Available in various specialized forms, the garden furniture maker will be concerned with three basic types, listed below. The material used for the handles is important, since they are both held in the hand and struck with a mallet (or less properly, a hammer) and so must be both comfortable and strong. Wooden handles are pleasant to hold, but fragile, whilst high-impact plastic is durable but uncomfortable.

Bevel-edged Chisels

These are the most common type on sale, but the bevelling of the edge makes them more suited to fine work (cabinet making, for example) than the type of use to which the garden furniture maker will put them. Pleasant for lighter work – *useful*.

Firmer Chisels

Differing from the bevel-edged variety only in that the edge is square. This makes the blade stronger and the square edge helps to guide the tool in mortises and so on – *essential*. A variation is the 'registered pattern', which has a heavier section and steel hoops fitted to the handle to prevent splitting when struck.

Sash Mortise Chisels

These are a long, heavy section chisel. Designed for chopping deep mortises, the length and strength of the blade enables it to be used as a lever, removing waste quickly. Hard to find nowadays – *luxury*.

MEASURING AND MARKING OUT TOOLS

All the tools in the world will not help if the job is not measured and marked out for cutting. Many of these tools are made of exotic timbers such as rosewood, and bound with brass – avoid these, beautiful though they are, as all wood moves with time, and rosewood more than most. The following is by no means a comprehensive list, but encompasses those which are relevant to this book's subject.

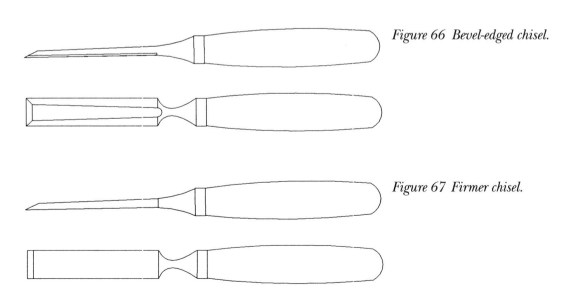

Figure 66 Bevel-edged chisel.

Figure 67 Firmer chisel.

TOOLS

Measuring

The ubiquitous tape measure is available in various lengths, but the most appropriate is the 5m (16ft), which also has a wider and therefore stronger tape than shorter models – *essential*. Look for a positive lock and a strong return spring, otherwise you could end up with a tape which either will not stay out, or will not go back. A 12in (300mm) steel rule should be used for shorter measuring – *useful*.

Squares and Bevels

As mentioned above, rosewood squares are unreliable, so only an all steel engineer's square can be relied on for total accuracy – *luxury*. Sliding, or adjustable, squares are useful for general work, and include a mitre (45 degree) angle and a 12in steel rule – *essential*. Sliding bevels are used to set and mark odd angles and again those with an alloy, or even plastic, body are more practical – *useful*.

Gauges

A marking gauge consists of a pin projecting from a stock, on which a block slides to be fixed at a variable distance from the pin – *essential*. These are used to mark lines parallel with an edge and are all made of hardwood. A mortise gauge differs in that it has a second pin fixed to a sliding member in the stock and is used to mark out pairs of lines, as are required for mortises – *useful*.

EVERYTHING ELSE

While the main primary tools are covered above, there are hundreds more which have been left out – these include

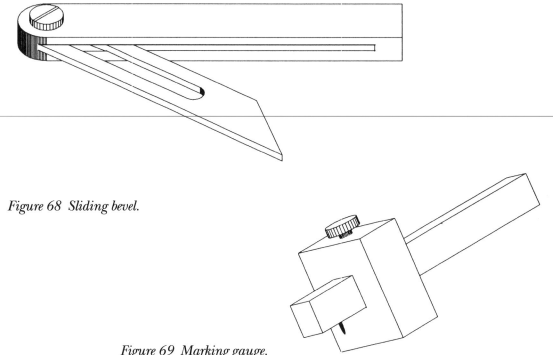

Figure 68 Sliding bevel.

Figure 69 Marking gauge.

screwdrivers, hammers and mallets as well as some much more obscure items. It is simply not possible to list them all in a single chapter, but the suggested tool kits below will contain those most likely to be needed, others are introduced in the chapter on techniques. Further reading for those wishing to know more includes manufacturer's and mail order catalogues, as well as the several books available on the subject of woodworking tools. Browsing in the better stocked tool shops can also be educational, as handling an unfamiliar tool can explain its purpose and operation more effectively than the written word.

When building up a set of tools, the best plan is to buy them as they are needed. In this way 'white elephants' will be avoided – shiny and complicated pieces of equipment which look as though they will be useful, but which somehow never get used.

Always buy the best quality you can afford. It is better to have a few good tools than a lot of indifferent ones. Good tools should last a lifetime if cared for, will improve the quality of your work and will not let you down at the crucial moment.

SUGGESTED TOOL KITS

The Bare Essentials

hardpoint saw
coping saw
bowsaw
hacksaw
jack plane
spokeshave
brace and wheel brace or cordless drill
set of lip and spur drills
auger drills as necessary
set of firmer chisels
    (with shatter-proof handles)
claw hammer
5m (16ft) tape measure
Stanley knife
marking gauge
adjustable square

flat blade and Phillips screwdrivers and/or screwdriver bit set for cordless drill
300mm (12in) spirit level

A More Comprehensive Kit Might Comprise

All of the above, plus:
tenon saw
jigsaw
smoothing plane
block plane
power drill
small sizes of HSS twist drills
random orbital sander
two or three bevel-edged chisels
300mm (12in) steel rule
sliding bevel
mortise gauge
1m (3ft) spirit level

Abrasives, Adhesives and Fixings

At first sight this seems a disparate collection of headings, having little to do with each other. In fact they sit together rather well – they will all be bought from the same type of supplier and they are all 'consumable' in the sense that they are used up in the course of the work. They also tend to be an afterthought; bought hastily at the last minute (which invariably means late on a Saturday afternoon). Choosing these important components on the basis of which shop is still open does not allow much scope for careful consideration.

This has a detrimental effect on the quality of the finished article, which is a shame as a little planning is all that is needed. There are things which will be used in all woodworking projects, and carrying a small stock of these basics does not involve a significant investment – it will also mean more time for making the garden furniture and less spent wandering forlornly up and down the aisles of the local DIY superstore!

ABRASIVES

Note that the word 'sandpaper' is not used. Sandpaper (literally grains of sand stuck onto a paper backing, with an animal glue) has long been superseded by glasspaper, which is the pale yellow, crinkly stuff familiar to most of us. Glasspaper is of little use, however, as it is too 'friable' (wears out too quickly) and prone to clogging.

Modern abrasives represent a good deal of engineering research and have been refined into various grades, not just of coarseness, each having specific characteristics. The factors which affect the performance of an abrasive are: grit size, particle type, and backing material (type and weight).

Grit Size

The terms 'coarse, medium and fine' are not really meaningful – what is coarse to one might be medium to another. Grits are better graded according to how many occur in a given area of the paper, and thus the following sizes are used:

36 grit
50 grit
80 grit
120 grit
240 grit
320 grit
400 grit

The smaller the number, the coarser the abrasive. Many other numbers will be seen, partly because there are two standards of classification used – one European and one American – but by and large it is a reliable indication of relative coarseness. Most woodworkers will find that they use abrasives in the range 80 to 240 grit, unless deliberately using an abrasive for shaping, in which case the lower grades will remove stock at quite a rate.

Particle Type

All kinds of materials have been, and are, used for the abrasive grits, from shark skin in the eighteenth century to diamond. Glass has already been discounted, and the remaining materials useful to our purpose are emery, aluminium oxide, and silicon carbide. Emery is largely the preserve of the metalworker, usually bonded to a cloth backing, and silicon carbide is the particle used in wet and dry paper, much used for cutting back lacquer and paint finishes. The most common type for woodworking abrasives is aluminium oxide, which is a strong and durable substance. It is available in sheet form or as a 50m roll, which although initially more costly to buy is much cheaper per square foot. The better type of supplier will offer this material in either open or close coated form. Of the two, open coated is better suited to softwoods as it is less prone to clogging by resin, whereas close coated abrasives will give a smoother finish.

Backing Type

Three options will be presented, being cloth, paper or Velcro. Cloth is used more for sanding belts for machine or power sanders, as is Velcro backing. Many orbital and all random orbital sanders use Velcro-backed paper, allowing it to be securely fixed, yet easily removable. The abrasive must be purchased in pre-cut shapes (often with punched holes for dust-collection systems) which at first sight is a very expensive option, but in practise works well, as the papers are easily reusable. This means that one can 'work through the grades' with a power sander, using first 80 grit, then 120 grit, finishing off with 240 grit, without discarding each piece of abrasive each time the grade is changed. For hand sanding a paper backing is used, a lighter paper for shaped work where its flexibility is needed and heavier for flat surfaces.

ADHESIVES

Adhesives are of lesser importance for the maker of garden furniture than for most woodworkers. This is because such work

lives out of doors and adhesives cannot be expected to survive such conditions indefinitely, and consequently garden furniture is assembled using largely 'mechanical' means of attaching one piece to another. This does not mean that metal fittings are necessarily involved, but that a joint will hold together by the fitting of the components to each other, so that any glue used is there to 'set' something that is already fixed. This is not to say that adhesives are not important even in exterior work, but that they must not be used instead of a good joint.

The exception to this is where there is a large gluing area in relation to the size of the components. When laminating two or more pieces together to form a curve, there is no mechanical method. The gluing area is large and a good waterproof adhesive may be used here with confidence. If there is a rule for this, it might be that the gluing area must be the largest dimension of the pieces to be glued. Following this rule, it will be seen that gluing a number of boards together face-to-face to form a table support will probably be successful, while gluing two or three boards edge-to-edge for the top will fail, unless a mechanical joint is used.

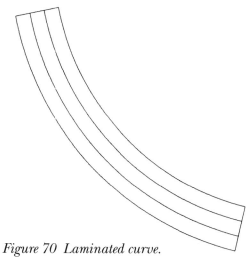

Figure 70 Laminated curve.

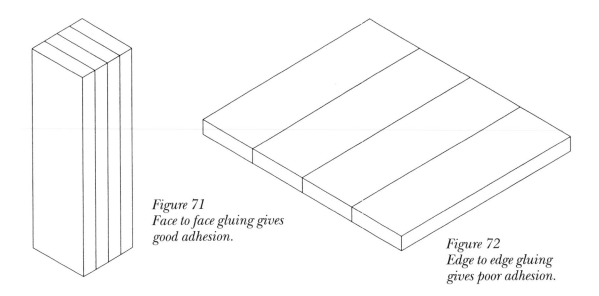

Figure 71
Face to face gluing gives
good adhesion.

Figure 72
Edge to edge gluing
gives poor adhesion.

Commonly available adhesives which are suitable for exterior woodwork include 'waterproof', or more correctly water resistant, cross-linking polyvinyl acetate (PVA). This should not be confused with the familiar 'white glue' (also polyvinyl acetate) which has no water resistance – this type of glue sets by losing moisture and will come unstuck on being exposed to damp.

The highest performance adhesive likely to be found for exterior work is the resinorcal formaldehyde type. This glue is used in building the type of boat that spends all of its time in water (as opposed to being kept on hardstanding between use) and may be regarded as waterproof, but might take a little finding.

Easy to obtain and almost as good as this latter adhesive is the urea formaldehyde type, widely sold under the name of Cascamite. This glue is again used in boat-building, although not recommended for permanent immersion, and should be the standard adhesive for the garden furniture maker. It is bought in the form of a white powder, which is mixed with water in precise proportions for use – it must be kept dry when stored, otherwise all you will have

is a solid block! Once mixed, it should be applied to the joint and clamped within about twenty minutes, and then kept under pressure for at least two hours. Clamping times will be considerably longer in cold weather and it pays to warm the timber before gluing in winter.

It should be noted that all adhesives contain chemicals which may carry a health risk and the maker's instructions for handling should be followed carefully, although exposure to non-industrial quantities is unlikely to pose a significant threat.

FIXINGS

Covered by this category are all the forms of metal fixings used in woodworking, being primarily nails, woodscrews and bolts. Using these is not an admission of failure by the woodworker, but a practical way of fixing one piece of wood to another. It has the advantage of being an instant joining method, with no waiting for glue to dry. In this way a complicated structure (such as a trellis) may be built up piece by piece quite quickly. This is also likely to be the primary method of joining for rustic work, as uneven pieces may be securely fixed with a nail or a screw where no gluing surface exists and the cutting of a joint would interfere with the look of the piece. A further benefit exists when using nuts and bolts in that a structure (whether it is a table, an arbor or a bridge) can be prepared in a workshop, garage or shed for assembly in its intended location, and can be taken apart for storage or to be moved.

Nails

Of the many types of nail available, the two which will find a use in garden furniture are the round and oval wire variety. The name describes the cross-section of the nail, the round wire nail also having a head which prevents it from being driven below the surface of the timber. The oval nail, if used with the direction of the grain, is less likely to cause a split to develop. As these have no large head, they may be punched below the surface of the timber and the hole filled, concealing the nail. One drawback of this is that the nail may also be pulled right through the wood, causing the joint to fail and making oval wires unsuitable for heavy work, or for a trellis where the nail must act as a pivot. Ordinary steel nails of either type will rust quickly if used outdoors, so the galvanized type should be used. Oak will react with the iron in a steel nail, corroding it and producing a black stain. Copper nails can be found (albeit with some difficulty) for use with oak, but are too soft to be driven directly into the timber, and so must be driven into pre-drilled holes. Oak is so resistant to nailing that this would probably also be necessary with steel nails.

Woodscrews

Woodscrews are identified by the shape of the head, the type of thread, and the material from which they are made, together with any plating applied. The traditional slotted

head is falling out of favour, particularly as the cross-headed screw is better suited to being driven by a cordless or power drill – often without the need to drill a pilot hole. Having said this, the round-headed, slotted screw is very good for attaching hardware, and looks right! Countersunk headed screws will be flush with the surface of the timber when driven, giving both a neat appearance and a surface free from projections. If this type of screw is to be withdrawn (to disassemble a piece of furniture for storage, for example) then it can be used with a cup washer. This is a socket-type washer into which the countersunk head fits.

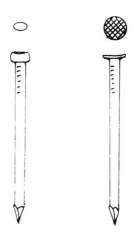

Figure 73 Oval wire (left) and round wire nails.

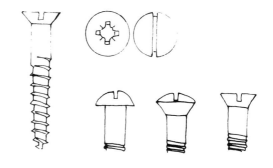

Figure 74 Types of woodscrew.

Woodscrews are available in mild steel (generally only with slotted heads), brass and hardened, zinc-plated. The plain steel woodscrew will soon be a thing of the past, as the demand for them has dropped in favour of the hardened zinc-plated type. This latter is the more suitable for exterior use anyway, for the same reason as galvanized nails. Hardened screws have very sharp points and threads and this combines with the lack of a plain shank to make them easy to drive, under power, without a pilot hole. The drawback is that hardened steel is more brittle and therefore likely to snap, so pilot holes are advisable in hard timbers.

Brass screws (or hardened brass-plated) should be used in oak to avoid iron-stain. As with copper nails, a pilot hole must be drilled and threads cut with a steel screw of the same size.

Screw sizes are currently in transition from the old, imperial measurement of diameter number (4, 6, 8, 10, 12, etc.) and length in fractional inches to metric diameter and length. Thus a 2in, number eight woodscrew is now referred to as a 4/50mm.

Bolts

As previously mentioned, bolts can be used where a structure is to be assembled on site, and where it may need to be taken apart at a later date. The principle bolt used for such purposes is the coach bolt, which has a round head with a square flange beneath it. This means that only one spanner is needed to tighten a coach bolt, as the square flange sinks into the timber and is prevented from rotating. A washer should always be used between the timber and the nut, so that this part does not sink in. Coach bolts are available in plain steel, galvanized steel, and zinc-plated (*see* comments for such types under nails and screws). Whilst not strictly a bolt, a coach screw is used for similar purposes – it is a heavy duty woodscrew with a square head.

Figure 75 Coach bolt.

Any type of bolt can be pressed into service, and threaded rod (known as studding) is useful. Studding is sold in lengths of up to 4ft (1200mm) and is cut to size to suit the job. A nut and washer is used at each end.

HARDWARE

Many pieces of outdoor furniture make use of metal brackets in the construction. A range of these will be found in most ironmongers and builder's merchants, and they may be modified to suit with a hacksaw and a drill. Avoid the flimsier types and try to buy those with some kind of galvanized or plated finish, although this will be spoiled rather if it is cut through. For a really special job, a blacksmith (there are more of these around than one would expect) will make up brackets, and these can make an effective design feature in themselves. If hinges are to be used the same considerations apply as to brackets; use a slightly larger size than is really needed for long term reliability and avoid the thin, pressed mild steel type – these will not last.

SUPPLIERS

The DIY superstore offers a limited range of the items mentioned in this chapter, and often at quite high prices. Builder's merchants will stock some, especially nails, screws and bolts, as will a good tool shop, but what is really needed is an old-fashioned ironmongers. If you are fortunate enough to have one of these excellent shops nearby then patronise it as much as possible and persuade your friends to do likewise.

Techniques

Having obtained the tools and the timber, the next step is to apply the one to the other – or so it would seem. In fact there is a little more planning to be done first.

WORKING AREA

Whether you will be working in a heated double garage or on a patio between rainstorms, it is worth thinking of it as a workplace. This should suggest a bench or worktop, somewhere to keep materials and a place for tools. The itinerant woodworker has to use some ingenuity to achieve this, but the considerations are the same. A secure working surface with some means of holding a piece of timber is a must – it is impossible to even cut a piece of wood that is wobbling around, let alone do so accurately, although fingers, hands and even legs cut quite easily in this situation.

The materials should be neatly stacked in such a way that the whole pile does not have to be moved to get at the piece required, and should be neither precarious nor in the way. Sharp-edged tools and concrete have a magnetic attraction for each other – it is always the chisel and never the hammer that falls onto the floor – so they must be kept neatly in a box or rack when not actually being used. Trailing leads from power tools are fond of tripping people up and more than one has been severed by the circular saw which it was supplying. It is a good idea to use an extension lead so that the plug and lead can be arranged behind the operator, and a circuit breaker should always be fitted to it. In this way whichever power tool is being used will be protected from damage to the lead or exposure to water, especially if working outside.

The minimum requirement, therefore, is a clear space to work in, a Workmate-type bench, a tool box and an extension lead fitted with a circuit breaker – whether these are used outside, in the garage or the living room.

PLANNING THE JOB

Resist the urge to start cutting for a little longer. It is easier to make a piece of wood smaller than larger, so make a drawing and a cutting list. The drawing need not be a masterpiece of draughtsmanship, as long as you understand it. A full-size drawing (a 'rod') can save a lot of confusion later. A sheet of hardboard makes an excellent surface for a rod as the pieces can be laid on it for checking, and it cannot be accidentally torn. A cutting list is simply a list of the individual pieces needed for the project, showing their quantity and dimensions. A cutting list for a slatted table might look like this:

Item	Length	Width	Thickness	No.	Material
Leg	700mm	50mm	50mm	4	Scots pine
Stretcher	850mm	40mm	20mm	4	Douglas fir
Rail	850mm	75mm	20mm	4	Douglas fir
Slats	920mm	40mm	20mm	16	Douglas fir
Battens	780mm	50mm	20mm	2	Douglas fir

This list will enable the woodworker to keep a constant check on the state of the job; as each piece is cut it can be ticked off in pencil, once it is planed it can be ticked in ink, and so on. Once each piece is complete it should be clearly marked – this would avoid any confusion between the stretchers and slats in the example given.

MEASURING AND MARKING OUT

Unless making a piece of fitted furniture (unusual in the garden) or perhaps an arbour which must fit exactly between two walls, then accuracy of measurement need not be 'absolute'. This apparent heresy does not mean that sloppiness is acceptable, but that 'relative' measurement is more important. Let us take, for example, four legs for a table which our drawing and cutting list tell us should be 700mm long. It is much better that they are all 705mm long than that one is 700mm, one 702mm, the third 699mm, and the fourth 701mm. Unless we can guarantee repeatable accuracy when marking out we should clamp them all together and

mark them out as one piece – possibly even cut them in the same way. Another approach would be to cut the first, then mark the others from it, although this is not quite as reliable. As the project takes shape, cut further parts to fit those which are finished, rather than sticking rigidly to the cutting list – well-fitting joints are more important than a 5mm discrepancy in the length of a bench, especially if no one else knows how long it was supposed to be!

Measure carefully and then do it again to check. Only use a pencil for general work, never for marking out a joint, as the thickness of a pencil line is too vague and hard to follow. Instead, use a knife for critical work. Most of this will be done with a steel square, which should be held firmly, and the knife drawn lightly along it, as if too much pressure is applied it may wander off on its own. The same applies to the marking gauge, which should be drawn firmly along the edge of the work but without undue pressure. The stock and fence of the gauge maintain contact with the timber and the pin just scores the surface.

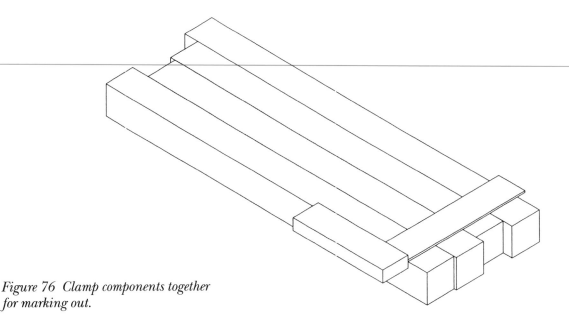

Figure 76 Clamp components together for marking out.

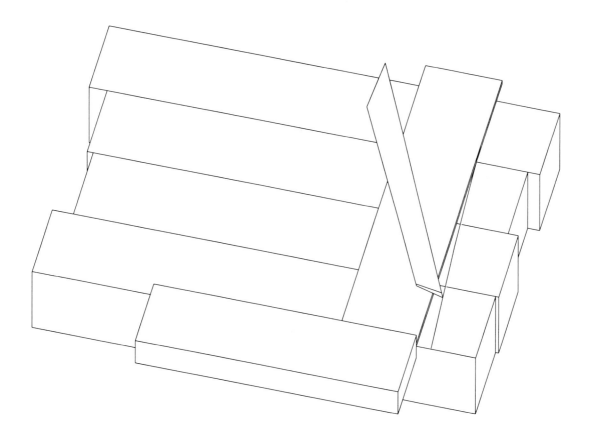

Figure 77 Too much pressure on the marking knife causes it to wander.

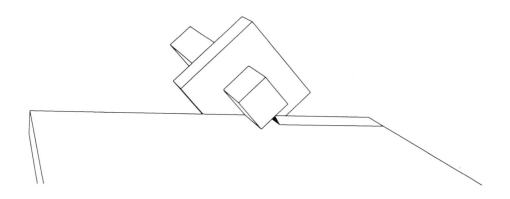

Figure 78 The body of the marking gauge maintains contact with the face.

SAWING

As previously stated, the first tool to touch the timber (after the marking knife) is the saw – and it may be the last. It is possible to correct a poorly executed saw cut with the block plane or chisel, but this takes up a lot of time and effort, whereas a job will take no time at all if good, accurate sawing is maintained. It will be seen then that this is a technique worth mastering.

Hand Sawing

The blade of a handsaw is a large flat surface with teeth along one edge. The teeth do the cutting, but the flat surface does the guiding. Once the cut is started, the saw will be kept to the line, more or less, by the blade being supported in the cut. This means that the cut must be started accurately, with the blade being square to the timber in both the vertical and lateral planes. Once started, the saw should be allowed to cut largely by its own weight, as 'forcing' the saw will cause it to wander. The job of the operator is to move the saw back and forth, using its full length, and to see that it stays in line letting the teeth cut freely – press hard and the teeth will dig in too far.

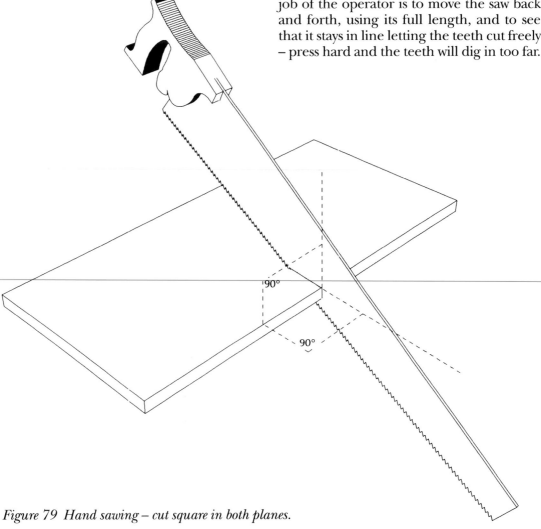

Figure 79 Hand sawing – cut square in both planes.

If the saw will not cut if used in this way, then it is not sharp enough, or of the wrong type for the cut (*see* Chapter 4 on tools). Do not try to saw down the middle of a marked line, but to one side of it – it may be helpful to mark two parallel lines the width of the saw cut, or 'kerf', and to saw between these. Hold the saw firmly with the index finger pointing along the blade, and do not move the wrist or elbow except to change direction, the power coming from the shoulder. Support the work on both sides of the cut, as it is not possible to cut a straight line in a piece of wood that is wobbling, and much more effort is needed.

When sawing along the grain it is useful to think of the 'drinking straw' structure of the wood, illustrated in the chapter on timber. This means that the saw will have a tendency to follow the grain, and that the 'sawdust' produced will be longish strings of fibre rather than a dust. To cut in this way the saw must be very sharp as it is cutting the fibres diagonally, it should also have a fairly deep 'gullet' between the teeth to avoid being clogged by the strings of fibre.

Cutting across the grain is easier in terms of both effort and accuracy, as the

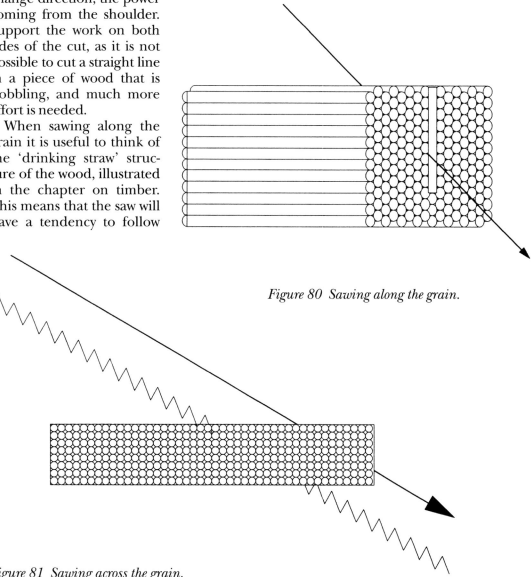

Figure 80 Sawing along the grain.

Figure 81 Sawing across the grain.

saw is cutting across the fibres. The ends of the severed fibres are too short to force the saw off its intended line and a fine dust is produced which clears the cut readily, therefore allowing a finer saw to be used without clogging.

If a sharp, straight saw tends to jam in a cut (with or across the grain) then a little wax applied to the blade (not the teeth!) will help. If problems are still encountered then too much pressure is being used, indicating that the saw is not as sharp as was thought. It may also be, in the case of rip cuts, that the cut is closing and pinching the blade.

Powered Sawing

Much the same advice applies to using power saws – do not force the cut but allow the saw to do the cutting and concentrate on guiding the saw. It is even more important that the work is securely held and that it is well supported on both sides of the cut.

A jigsaw blade will 'lean' if forced, especially when cutting curves, and patience at this stage will avoid a lot of corrective work later. Be sure that the right type of blade is fitted – few teeth and a deep gullet for ripping, otherwise overheating will occur shortening the life of the blade, and

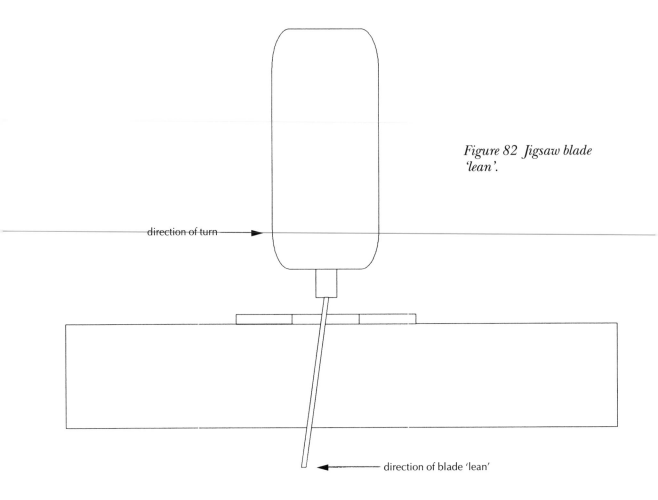

Figure 82 Jigsaw blade 'lean'.

direction of turn →

← direction of blade 'lean'

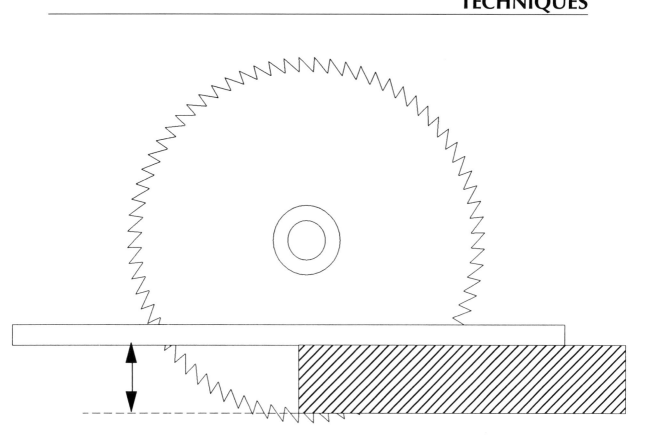

Figure 83 Adjust the depth of cut of a circular saw.

more teeth for cross-cutting will give a cleaner finish.

The depth of cut of a circular saw should be adjusted so that it is no greater than is necessary. Whereas the jigsaw is normally used 'freehand', guided along a line by the operator, the circular saw should ideally be restrained in its direction by some sort of guide. The fence supplied with these machines is useful for ripping if a straight edge already exists, but generally guiding the baseplate of the saw along a straight edge clamped to the work will be successful. The implications of jamming in the cut are quite serious in the case of the circular saw, as the power that was spinning the blade will be re-directed. This can cause the saw to jump out of the

cut altogether – clearly a dangerous occurrence. Jamming will be caused by the blade being pinched in a closing cut, which can happen in two circumstances. First, when cross-cutting a piece of wood that is not supported correctly, the free end may drop, or the board may sag at the cut. Avoid this by taking care to support the work properly at both sides of the cut and think about the change in balance as the cut is made. Secondly, when ripping, tensions in the wood may be released, causing the cut to close up behind the saw. This may be avoided by placing wedges in the cut to hold it apart. This should be done by an assistant while the cut is being made, as the saw must not be stopped and re-started in the cut or it may jump.

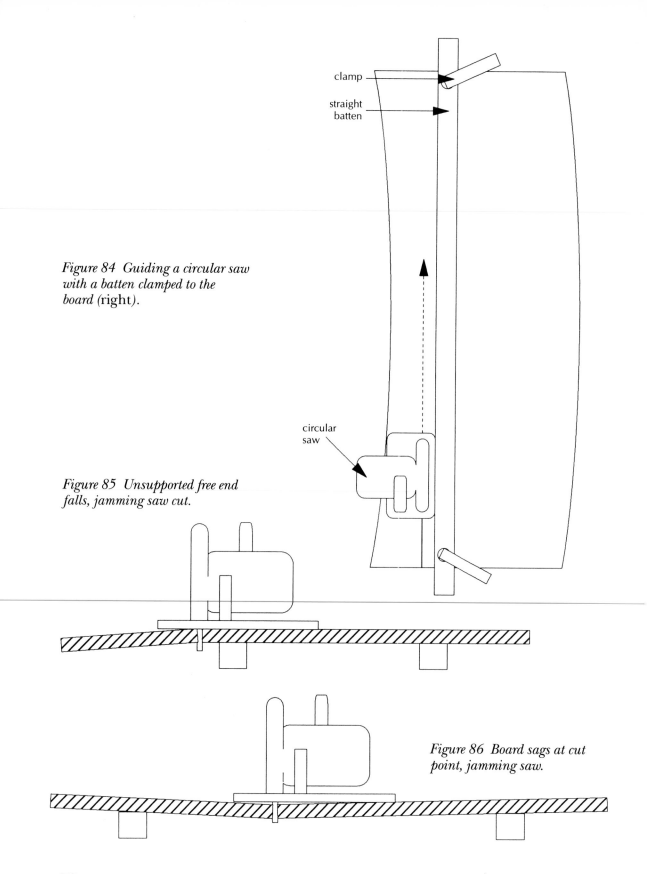

clamp

straight
batten

*Figure 84 Guiding a circular saw
with a batten clamped to the
board* (right).

circular
saw

*Figure 85 Unsupported free end
falls, jamming saw cut.*

*Figure 86 Board sags at cut
point, jamming saw.*

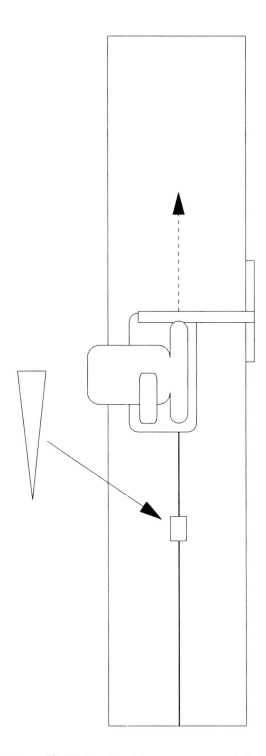

PLANING

This is the operation which seems to hold the most mystery for the beginner. Perhaps this is because success or failure are determined by the relationship between a number of factors, from setting up the plane in the first place to the direction in which it is applied. First we will look at the plane itself, and how to set it.

The Bailey-pattern hand plane consists of a cast iron body, the 'frog' which carries the adjustments, the cutting iron (the 'blade'), the cap iron which reinforces the cutting iron and acts as a chip breaker, the lever cap which holds the cutting and cap irons in place, and a couple of handles. This represents quite a lot of components for a single tool, and with the exception of the handles everything must be properly adjusted for successful planing to take place.

Fresh from the box a plane will be almost usable, but we can improve on that quite easily. First the cutting iron must be sharpened (*see* the section on sharpening at the end of this chapter). Next the mouth is set

Figure 87 Wedge placed in cut to prevent closing.   *Figure 88 Bailey-pattern hand plane.*

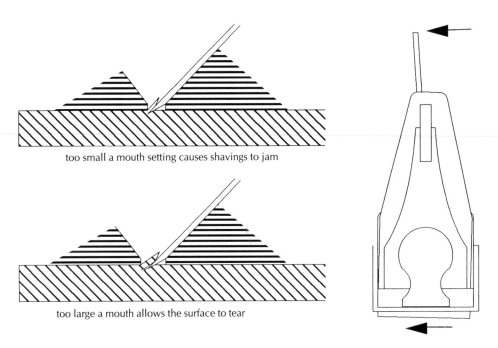

too small a mouth setting causes shavings to jam

too large a mouth allows the surface to tear

Figure 89 Setting the mouth.

Figure 90 Angling the plane iron (above).

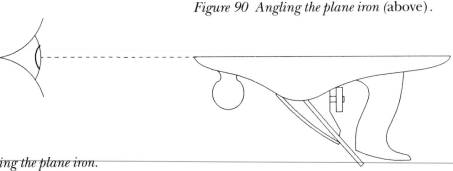

Figure 91 Setting the plane iron.

–this is done by slackening the screws fixing the frog to the body, and adjusting the frog setting screw to give a mouth gap (with the cutting and cap irons fitted) of around 2.5mm for general work. Too small a mouth will result in the shavings becoming jammed in the mouth and too large a mouth will allow the fibres to tear.

Next the cap iron should be fixed to the iron, the critical measurement being the amount by which it is set back from the cutting edge. Again this distance should

be small for fine work and large for coarse — a good average is 1mm. Now reassemble the plane by fixing the cutting and cap irons in place with the lever cap.

The projection of the cutting iron from the body is adjustable in two directions: first depth of cut which is adjusted with the large brass thumb wheel behind the frog. This is turned clockwise to reduce the depth of cut, and counter-clockwise to increase it. The last turn made should always be counter-clockwise, or the cutting iron will slip upwards to take up the slack in the adjustment. The second adjustment is for the angle at which the cutting iron sits and is made with the lateral lever sticking out of the top. Moving this lever to one side will increase the projection of the cutter on the other. Make these adjustments whilst sighting down the sole of the plane, from which viewpoint the cutting iron will appear as a thin dark line. Aim to make this line parallel to the sole of the plane; the correct amount of projection will be learned through trial and error.

Now that the plane is ready for use, consider the direction of the grain in the piece to be planed. Back to those drinking straws again here – planing into the ends of the fibres will cause them to tear, so we must plane 'uphill'. Look at the side of the wood to determine the correct direction and if this is not clear, a couple of trial strokes will soon demonstrate if all is well.

At last we can start planing. The work must be securely held and supported on a bench or other stable surface, as it will bend away from the pressure of the plane otherwise and slipping will render planing impossible. A vice is not always the best work-holding device for planing; often a 'stop' fixed to the bench top will be better. Use your body weight to exert downward pressure onto the plane. At the start of the cut put the pressure on the front handle of the plane, during the cut make it even between the two handles, and at the finish the weight should be at the back. This will help to avoid 'rounding' the work. Do not draw the plane backwards along the work between strokes unless you enjoy sharpening, instead lift it off and start each stroke anew. If the timber is especially uneven, do not plane from one end to the other but instead take off the high spots first.

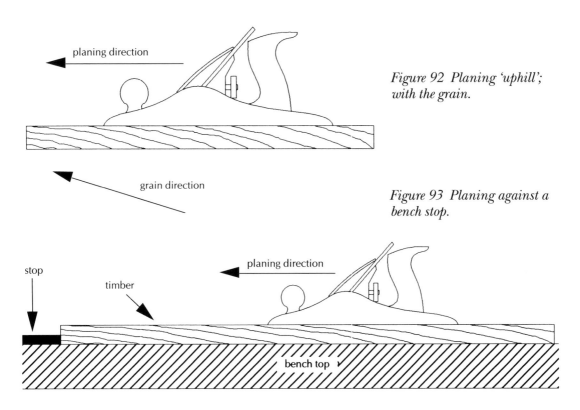

*Figure 92 Planing 'uphill';
with the grain.*

*Figure 93 Planing against a
bench stop.*

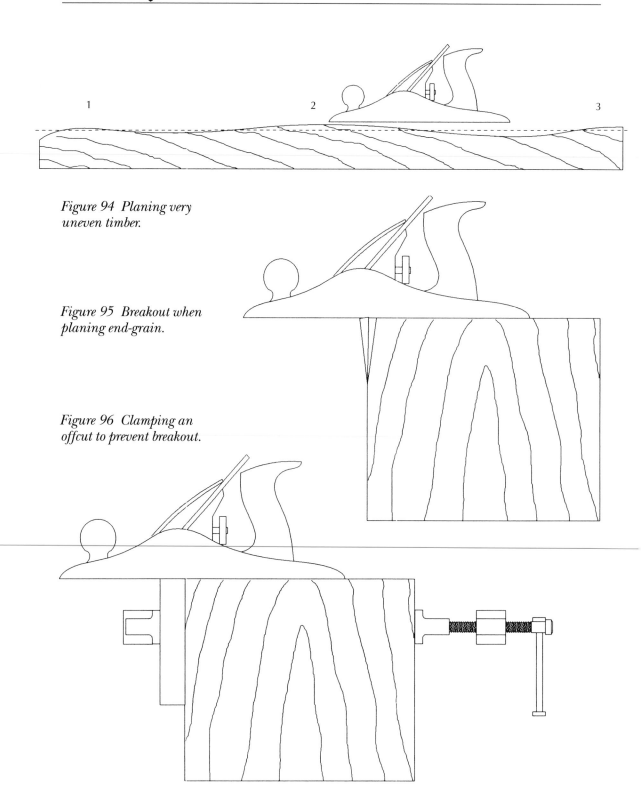

Figure 94 Planing very uneven timber.

Figure 95 Breakout when planing end-grain.

Figure 96 Clamping an offcut to prevent breakout.

Once the timber is more or less straight, then a full stroke or two will level any minor irregularities.

When planing the edge of a board, slip the fingers of the left hand underneath the plane to act as a fence and apply downward pressure in the area of the front handle with the thumb of the left hand – this helps to stop tilting when balancing the plane on a narrow edge. Check the edge for 'square' every couple of strokes and do so over the whole length, correcting any discrepancy by adjusting the pressure on the plane. If your 'out of square' is consistently to one side, then adjusting the lateral lever on the plane might help, but do not use this to compensate for uneven application of pressure.

When planing end grain, the cutting iron must be adjusted for a very fine cut. Remembering the drinking straws, it will be seen that the end of the cut will result in 'break out' if the fibres are unsupported. To prevent this, clamp a piece of scrap to the timber at the end of the cut. As with sawing across the grain, it is better to work to a knifed line than one drawn with a pencil, as this further reduces break out, and leaves a clean finish.

USING CHISELS

Blunt chisels cause a lot of accidents – many more than sharp ones. A blunt tool requires much more force to cut and in the case of a chisel this means pushing hard against the end of the handle. If anything goes wrong (and it usually does if corners are being cut) then all that force is released, causing the chisel to shoot forwards at speed, usually into some part of the body which you would prefer to leave intact. With a well-sharpened chisel, paring cuts may be made with minimal pressure, which allows greater control. It is wiser in any case to take a series of small cuts than one big one which requires undue force.

Two kinds of cut may be made with a chisel, paring and chopping. The former are made with hand pressure and usually along the grain. The comments regarding planing and grain direction apply equally to chisels: work 'uphill' and diagonally through the fibres rather than against them. When paring, the right hand should be on the handle, applying light forward pressure, and the left hand on the work; apart from the thumb of the left hand

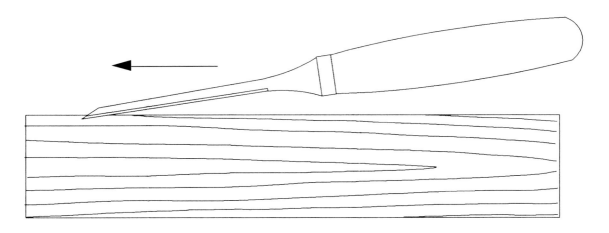

Figure 97 Paring with the grain.

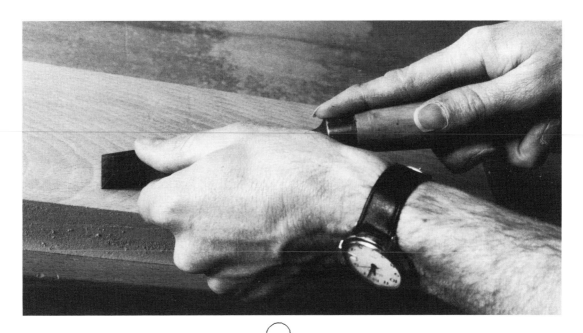

which will be applying downward pressure and guidance just behind the cutting edge of the chisel. This approach places both hands out of the path of the cutting edge, which is how it should be.

Chopping cuts are made mostly across the grain, for example when cutting a mortise. These cuts are best made using a mallet to provide the pushing force, as a short sharp cut will shear cut the fibres more cleanly than even pressure. Once again chopping cuts with a chisel should be marked out with a knife, which gives a clear line to work to. The chisel is held in the left hand, the right wielding the mallet. There should be no need to swing the mallet like an axe, a series of

Figure 98 Correct hand positions for paring (above).

Figure 99 Chopping – too heavy a cut.

wedge shape
forces chisel
to undercut

sharp, positive blows will be more controllable. Do not attempt to remove too much stock with one cut – this will cause the chisel to 'undercut' because of the wedge-shaped bevel . Better to work back to a line, which also allows for adjustments to the grip to be made for a square cut.

DRILLING

A large part of successful drilling is a matter of choosing the right drill and bit for the job in hand – refer to Chapter 4 on tools before proceeding. Small diameter (up to 8mm) holes in wood should be drilled at a relatively high speed using a lip and spur bit, and for this a power or cordless drill is as good as or better than a wheel brace. Larger diameter (8mm to 15mm) holes should be drilled at a slow to medium speed with an auger bit mounted in a cordless drill or a hand brace, while very large diameter (over 15mm) holes are also drilled with an auger

bit, but at a very slow speed. Obviously the type of material being drilled will have a bearing on what speed and type of drill is used for a given diameter, but if in doubt err on the side of caution – start slow.

Accuracy in marking out is particularly important when drilling holes which must correspond in multiple components, for example when bolting, dowelling or screwing parts together. Having measured and marked out as described above, mark the exact centre of each hole to be drilled using the point of a bradawl; the resulting small hole will provide a positive location for the centre point of a lip and spur or auger bit when starting and will reduce the risk of slipping.

Holes must not only start in the right place, but also finish where intended. This requires that the hole is drilled perpendicular to the surface – which is surprisingly difficult to achieve. When drilling a large number of holes which are especially critical, it may be worth considering using a power drill mounted in a drill stand, which will ensure that the holes are perpendicular. Since neither hand drills nor auger bits can be used in a drill stand, though, the following approach will be needed at least some of the time. Recruit an assistant, and have them watch the drill bit with their eye at the level of the work. They should be able to see if the drill is at right angles to the surface (standing a square on the work may help), and call out instructions as the hole is drilled. Practice helps and after a while it should be possible to drill holes that are fairly perpendicular without help.

Figure 100 Drilling at an angle prevents holes from lining up.

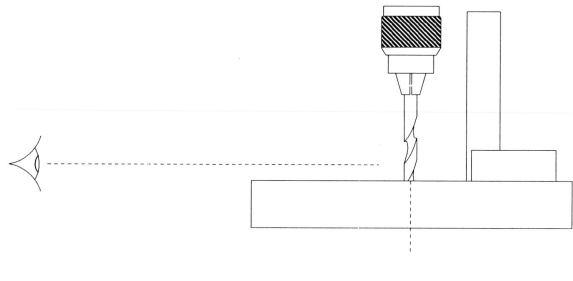

Figure 101 Perpendicular drilling by sighting.

Figure 102 Guiding an auger with a pilot hole.

The larger the diameter of the drill bit, the harder it is to keep in line. This is because the force needed to turn the bit takes all one's concentration, making it harder to control the direction of the drill. Before drilling a large diameter hole with an auger bit, drill a smaller 'pilot' hole. The point of the auger will tend to follow this hole, and provided that the pilot hole was perpendicular then the larger one should be, also.

SANDING

Abrasives perform two main functions for the woodworker; shaping and smoothing. In the case of the former, a coarse grit abrasive (*see* Chapter 5 on abrasives, adhesives and fixings) is used to remove relatively large amounts of timber, while in the case of the latter a finer grit is used to remove tool marks and smooth the surface for finishing. In neither case should the abrasive be used unsupported, since it is flexible

In the same way as marking out groups of components clamped together ensures relative accuracy, holes may be drilled through mating parts that are clamped together. Whilst this does not ensure that the hole is perpendicular, it does mean that the fit of the parts will not be spoiled if the drill does wander.

and will assume the shape of the finger – not a profile much used in woodwork!

The simplest form of support for abrasive is the simple wooden block shown in Chapter 4. This will not allow the paper to ride up and down over lumps on the wood, but like a plane will smooth the high spots leaving a level surface. If the paper tends to clog – most often seen on oily hardwoods like teak, and resinous softwoods such as pitch pine – then it may help to insert a piece of felt or leather between the paper and block, which will reduce the heat build-up. More complicated blocks may be made for specific tasks, such as rounding over corners. The heavier grades may also be stuck to metalworking files with double-sided tape for shaping work.

When shaping with abrasives it will be noted that stock removal is fastest when working across the grain. This is permissible, but remember that cross-grain scratches must be removed when the final sanding is done, so they are best kept to a minimum. Always use abrasives with a smooth, fluid motion; it is very easy to create a hollow or lump, but much harder to remove it. This is especially true when rounding over corners, which is probably how the threepenny bit was designed!

Final sanding must be done with the grain and with the longest strokes possible.

Persevere until all scratches are removed, particularly if a dark stain is to be used.

Powered Sanding

Everything that has been said about hand sanding applies equally to the use of powered sanders. These are great labour saving devices and if used with care will give excellent results and save time and effort. Beware, though, the speed with which things happen – a mistake takes no time at all to become a disaster! Always keep a sander moving, as it will create a hollow if left in one place.

Belt sanders are powerful shaping tools and will flatten an uneven surface reliably if they are kept moving. Keep the belt sander pointing in line with the grain, and use in a sweeping, circular motion on wide stock. If the timber to be sanded is narrow, then move the sander along it as you would a plane, setting down and lifting off at the start and finish of the 'cut'. Be careful not to tilt the sander on narrow stock – it may be necessary to clamp a scrap piece to the work to avoid this.

Orbital and random orbital sanders offer less scope for disaster, as they are primarily smoothing, rather than shaping, tools. Again, though, they must be kept moving if an uneven surface is to be avoided, using

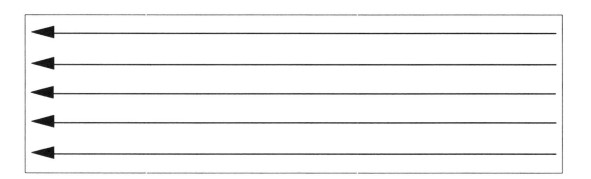

Figure 103 Sand with long strokes.

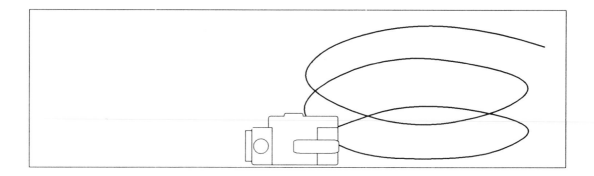

Figure 104 Use a belt sander in long oval strokes.

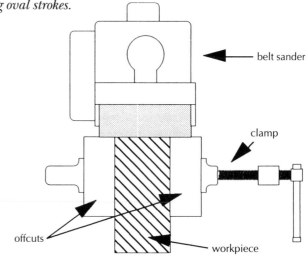

belt sander

clamp

offcuts

workpiece

Figure 105 Offcuts clamped to narrow workpiece to support sander.

the same circular motion as described for the belt sander, and never switch the sander on or off while it is resting on the work, or deep scratches will result.

SHARPENING

Nobody really enjoys sharpening tools – it is an interruption of the process of woodworking, rather than a part of it. As mentioned above, though, blunt tools are dangerous as they require more force to operate and however skilled the craftsman good work cannot be achieved without sharp tools.

The sharpening of hand saws is a delicate business and I am thankful to say that most tool shops can arrange for it to be done professionally at reasonable cost. Unless you feel a burning desire to sharpen your own saws, then take advantage of this service – if not, then describing the art is beyond the scope of this book and I humbly recommend that you seek out a specialist publication. Blades for jigsaws are disposable and circular saw blades, being tungsten carbide tipped, must be sharpened professionally.

This leaves us with chisels and plane irons, both of which are well within the scope of the amateur and which require the same approach. The first stage of sharpening is grinding, the process of removing metal to create the primary angle which is then honed to an edge. Grinding is carried out on a dry grinding wheel, driven at high speed by an electric motor. These are also available with a second wheel, rotating at a lower speed and lubricated with water. Dry grinding is not an easy process, especially of a wide blade such as a plane iron, as the blade must be moved across the face of the rotating wheel evenly, to grind a straight edge. If moved too slowly the edge will overheat, resulting in the loss of its ability to hold an edge. If this happens then the overheated area must be ground away. A guide of some kind is essential, as this will also hold the blade at a constant angle. Waterstones are easier to use as there is no possi-

bility of overheating, but they are much slower. If I am painting a gloomy picture of this process it is because the occasional user of tools should think long and hard before taking it on. Unless you are using your tools every day, then grinding will not be required more than once or twice a year and it is therefore probably cheaper, and certainly easier, to send your edge tools with the saw to be professionally ground. Honing is needed quite often, however, and the necessary equipment is limited to an oil stone and some light oil. First apply a little oil to the stone. An India carborundum stone will do a good job and last well, and general purpose (3 in 1 type) oil mixed half-and-half with white spirit is a good lubricant. Lay the back of the blade (the face which is not ground to an angle) on the

narrow grinding wheel

wide iron

Figure 106 Difficulty of grinding a plane iron.

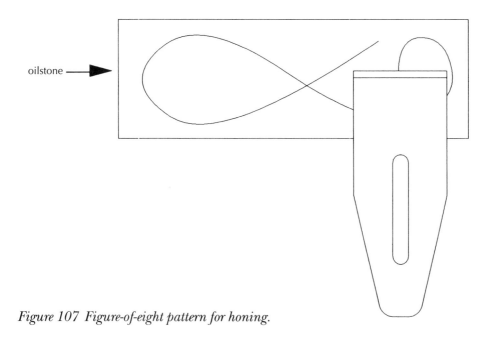

oilstone

Figure 107 Figure-of-eight pattern for honing.

stone and, pressing lightly downward, move it in a figure-of-eight pattern. Be careful to keep the blade flat, avoiding rocking. The aim is to flatten the back of the blade at the edge, indicated by a polished area. When the back is flat, the bevel may be ground.

Hold the blade bevel-side down with both hands at the required angle, thumbs below and fingers above the blade. Now move the blade in the same figure-of-eight pattern as used for the back; the tricky part is not to rock the blade as you do so. I find that keeping my wrists still, moving only my elbows and shoulders, does the trick, but there are many techniques – some keep their whole upper body still, moving from their knees – the important thing is to maintain the angle of the blade to the stone. When the bevel looks clean and polished, feel the edge from the back. A fine burr should be felt, if this runs the full length of the edge then turn the blade over and polish the back as before. The wire edge may fall off at this point, but if not then strop the edge by drawing it backwards over a piece of leather, front and back, until it is gone.

Sharpening angles vary according to the tool and the type of timber, but most workers will settle on a compromise which suits them. My own is the 25 degree grind with a 30 degree hone shown below. Several 'honing guides' are on the market whose chief purpose is to hold the tool at a set angle while it is sharpened, but they tend to accelerate the wear of the stone. It is easier to give a chisel a quick hone by hand and the easier it is, the more often it will be done!

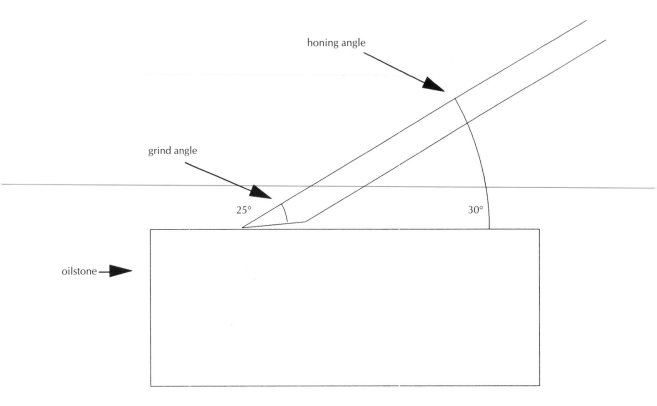

Figure 108 Honing at 30°, ground at 25°.

seven

Joints

The difference between a pile of wood and a garden bench is in the joints. To the newcomer, the reason for the multiplicity of joints in common use may seem obscure – surely no more than two or three are really needed? If we were working in anything other than timber then that would be the case, but given that our chief constructional material is a natural one, with the peculiar strengths, weaknesses and shrinkage characteristics described in the chapter on timber, then a range of joints are needed according to the situation. Choosing the right one is vital to the success and long-term durability of a project, so we will begin this chapter with a look at the different types of jointing situation and the different tasks that the joint is required to perform.

LOADS AND STRESSES

These may be classified as: compression (a pushing force), tension (a pulling force), torsion (a twisting force) and shear (a perpendicular force). Structural engineers will doubtless know of a few more, but these will do for our purposes.

Compression forces are usually supplied by gravity and a good example of a joint under compression is a stool's seat sitting on turned legs. Since things do not fall upwards, this joint can be as simple as a hole for the leg to fit in, and if the leg end and hole are tapered then this joint will be tightened by use although the wedging effect may split the seat. This is a very simple mortise and tenon joint, and it will be seen that a 'proper' tenon will better resist

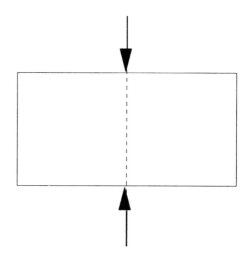

Figure 109 Compression force.

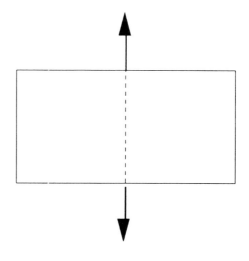

Figure 110 Tension force.

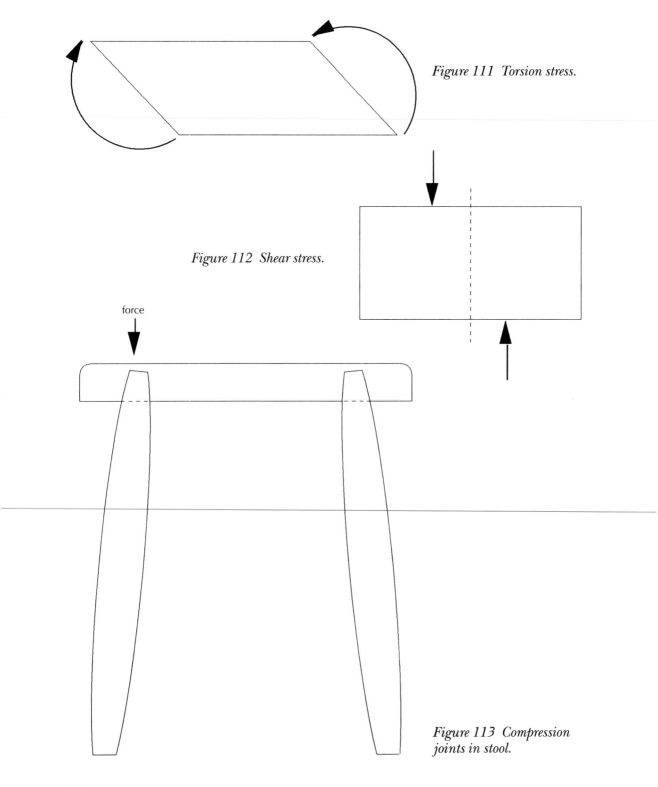

Figure 111 Torsion stress.

Figure 112 Shear stress.

force

*Figure 113 Compression
joints in stool.*

compression force tightens tapered leg in socket.

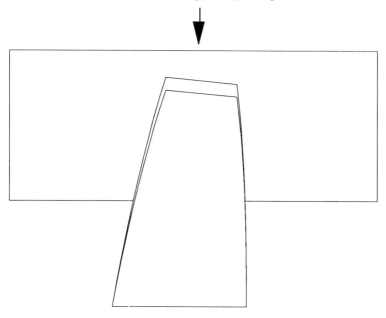

Figure 114 Compression joints in stool.

compression force

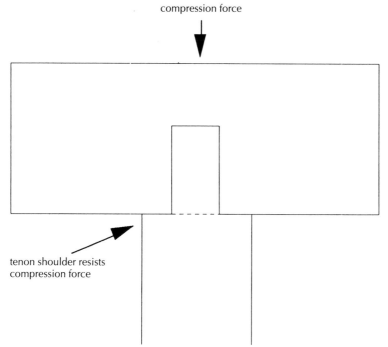

tenon shoulder resists
compression force

Figure 115 Tenons and compression.

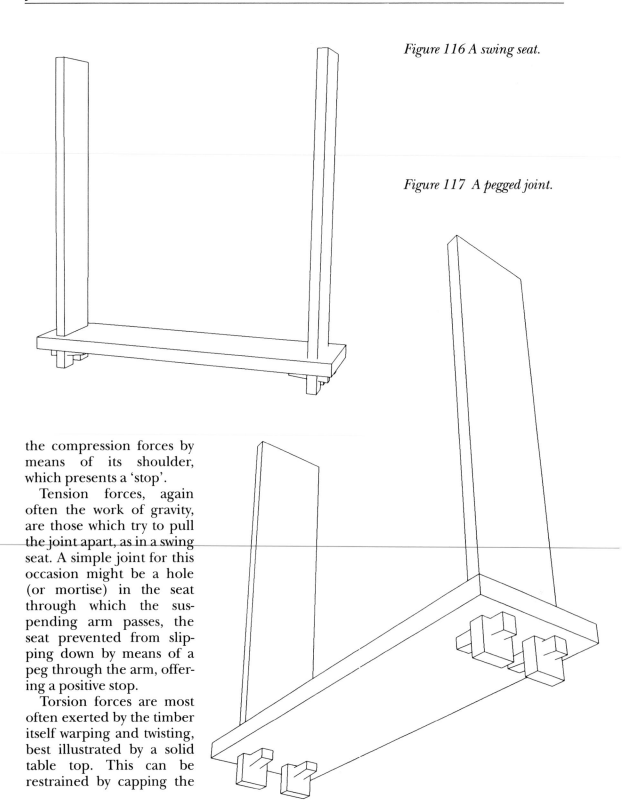

Figure 116 A swing seat.

Figure 117 A pegged joint.

the compression forces by means of its shoulder, which presents a 'stop'.

Tension forces, again often the work of gravity, are those which try to pull the joint apart, as in a swing seat. A simple joint for this occasion might be a hole (or mortise) in the seat through which the suspending arm passes, the seat prevented from slipping down by means of a peg through the arm, offering a positive stop.

Torsion forces are most often exerted by the timber itself warping and twisting, best illustrated by a solid table top. This can be restrained by capping the

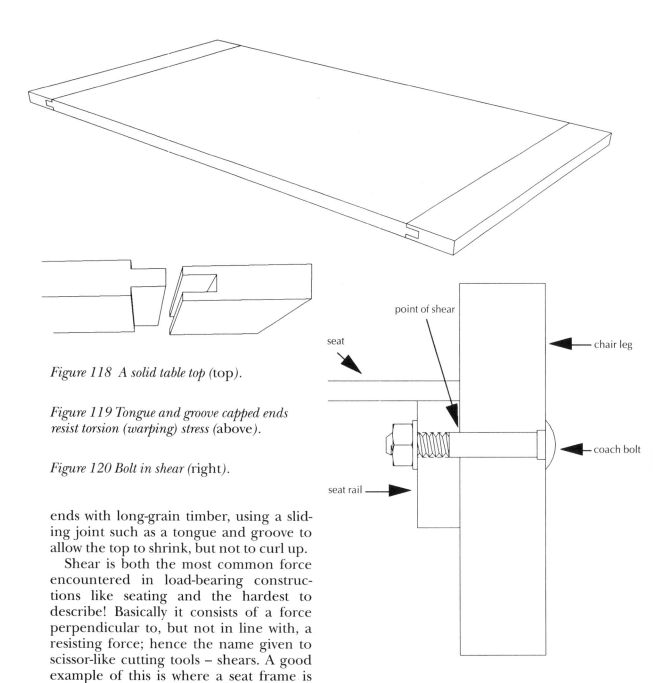

Figure 118 A solid table top (top).

Figure 119 Tongue and groove capped ends resist torsion (warping) stress (above).

Figure 120 Bolt in shear (right).

ends with long-grain timber, using a sliding joint such as a tongue and groove to allow the top to shrink, but not to curl up.

Shear is both the most common force encountered in load-bearing constructions like seating and the hardest to describe! Basically it consists of a force perpendicular to, but not in line with, a resisting force; hence the name given to scissor-like cutting tools – shears. A good example of this is where a seat frame is bolted to an upright from the side. The bolt in this example is 'in shear'.

Obviously a combination of these forces is likely to be present in a single piece of furniture, and even in a single joint. An awareness of them is very useful, however, in designing your projects and will help you to decide which joint is most appropriate for a given situation. They will be referred to as we look at individual joints and constructions.

JOINTS

NAILED JOINTS

Used for holding components together where they are not subject to severe tension or torsion, nailed joints have good resistance to shear and compression.

When nailing it is important that the work is well supported, as if it is able to 'bounce' a lot of the effort of striking the nail is wasted, and nails are more likely to bend if the work is moving. Although this is an 'ad hoc' joint requiring little preparation, it will often be necessary to clamp or otherwise firmly position the work if accuracy is to be maintained. This may be illustrated by a nailed trellis, which contains many nailed joints which also act as pivots. A jig will be required for this, to hold the pieces being nailed in exactly the right position. This kind of joint will have to be marked out just as carefully as a mortise and tenon, too.

In many hardwoods, especially oak, a pilot hole should be drilled to accept the nail otherwise the nail will bend or the timber may split – or both!

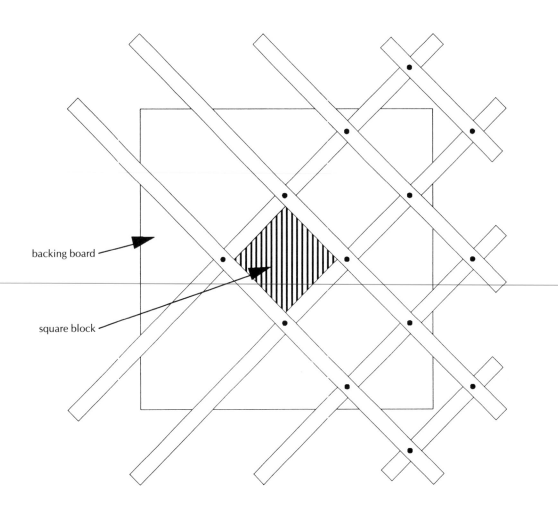

Figure 121 Nailing jig for trellis.

88

USE NAILS FOR:

Holding lightly stressed components in place, and restricting the movement of sound mechanical joints.

DO NOT USE NAILS FOR:

The sole means of effecting structural joints.

There are no prizes for driving in a nail with a single blow and a series of sharp taps will be more controllable. Hammers are designed quite carefully and you will find that holding them correctly at the end of the handle will give the right swing – avoid the tendency to move the hand progressively nearer the head of the hammer, as once again this will result in bent nails and frayed tempers.

SCREWED JOINTS

Used for holding moderately stressed components in place and where a joint may need to be taken apart. In many ways an improved nail, screwed joints have good resistance to shear and compression and some resistance to tension.

As there is no impact involved, screwed joints may be used where the work cannot be supported, or is too light to withstand a hammer blow – for example to assemble a light framework. With the exception of twin-start type screws driven under power with a cordless drill, the success of such a joint is dependent upon the accurate drilling of pilot and clearance holes.

A pilot hole is drilled both to guide the screw through the timber, and to remove some wood thus providing space for the screw to occupy. The size of a pilot hole should be roughly equal to the core of the screw – that is the diameter minus the thread. For softwood it should be a little smaller and hardwood a little larger. A clearance hole is one which the largest part of the screw will pass through.

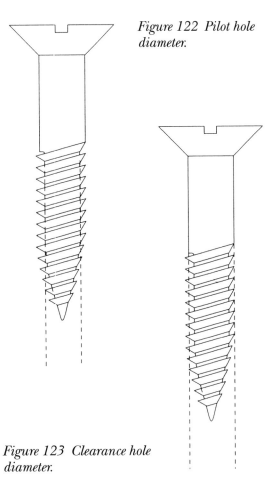

Figure 122 Pilot hole diameter.

Figure 123 Clearance hole diameter.

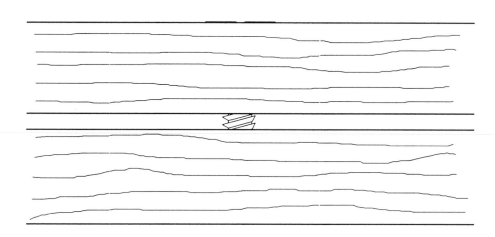

Figure 124 Joint held open by woodscrew.

USE SCREWS FOR:

Holding moderately stressed components in place, for light structural joints and where future dismantling is expected.

situation shown in Fig 124. For further advice regarding drilling, *see* Chapter 6 on techniques.

It is a good idea to lubricate screws with wax or similar, as this will not only aid the insertion (and avoid snapping the screw) but will ease later withdrawal. If the head of the screw becomes damaged whilst being driven by the use of a badly fitting screwdriver or too much force, then take it out and use a new one while you can – there is nothing so immovable as a screw without a slot and they always seem to give out before they are quite home!

When screwing one piece of wood to another, it is correct to drill a pilot hole in the bottom piece and a clearance hole (together with any countersinking or counterboring) in the top piece. In this way the screw will pull the joint together, whereas if a pilot hole only is drilled the screw may grip in both parts, and the joint could remain open even when the screw is fully driven. This is especially true when driving twin-start screws (which are threaded all the way to the head) without a pilot hole, using a cordless driver. If using this method, both parts must be clamped together to avoid the

DO NOT USE SCREWS FOR:

Medium or heavy structural joints.

BOLTED JOINTS

Used for holding moderately to heavily stressed components together, especially where: the joint may need to be taken apart; assembly is carried out on site using components prepared and test assembled elsewhere; and where other kinds of joint cannot be used due to an ungluable combination of material – for example wood to steel or brickwork. Bolted joints have good resistance to shear and compression and moderate resistance to tension and torsion provided that suitable washers are used. Bolts are therefore suitable for all kinds of joint from a structural point of view, but they are not attractive in themselves and so may be ruled out for some kinds of work on cosmetic grounds.

When assessing the suitability of a bolted joint, bear in mind that the bolt is probably stronger than the material being joined. If the hole required for the bolt is too large in relation to the sectional size of the material, it might weaken it to the point of fracture – so a huge bolt does not always mean a secure structure. Bear in mind also that the bolt head or nut can pull through timber, either when being tightened or when the joint is under stress in use. To minimize the risk of this happening a washer must be used under the nut and also under the head unless it is a coach bolt – the heads of these are designed to bed themselves in securely without a washer.

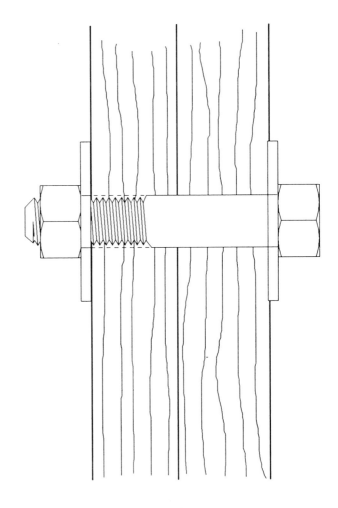

Figure 125 Using washers with bolts.

USE BOLTS FOR:

Forming moderately to heavily stressed structural joints, where prefabrication and later assembly is required, and where two or more incompatible materials are to be joined.

DO NOT USE BOLTS FOR:

Light sections of timber which may be weakened by the hole drilled for the bolt, or where a visible bolt would spoil the appearance of the project.

Making a successful bolted joint is almost entirely down to good drilling. When bolting two pieces of wood together, the aim should be to drill a clearance hole (*see* section on screwed joints) which lines up exactly in both pieces; both in terms of entry/exit point and direction. As the bolt will not bend to fit a kinked hole, the holes in both components must be drilled exactly perpendicular to the mating surfaces. Another way of dealing with this problem is to clamp both pieces together as they will be when joined and then drill through both components in one go; in most instances this is the best method to adopt.

Bolts are also used to supplement other types of joint – for example tenons and notched joints – as will be pointed out when these types of joint are discussed.

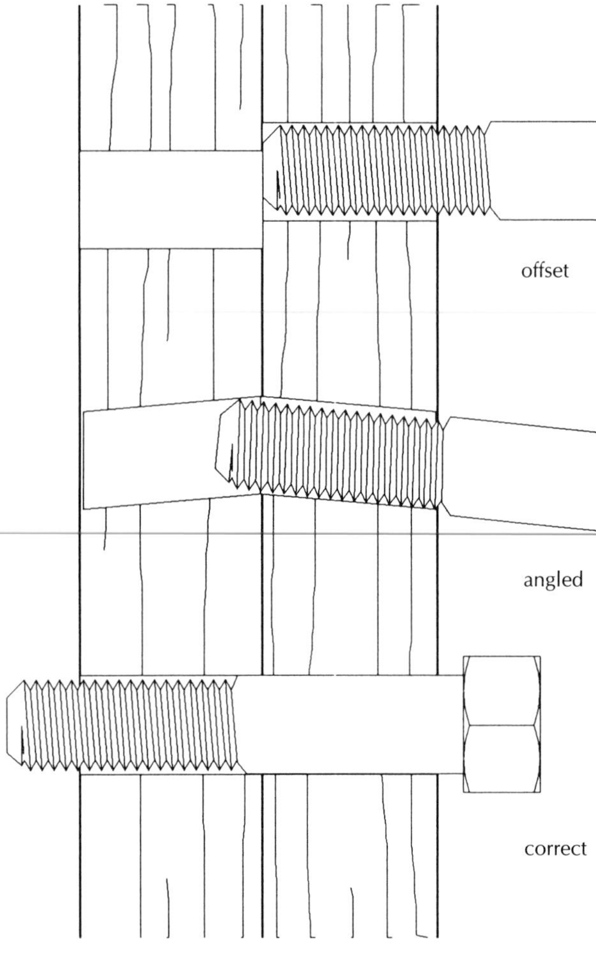

DOWELLED JOINTS

These are used for lightly stressed wood-to-wood joints where the joint will not have to be dismantled and to locate and reinforce an edge-to-edge glued joint. Dowelled joints have good resistance to compression, some resistance to shear and almost no resistance to tension or torsion.

Dowelled joints are easily made with very few tools being required – a drill, and measuring and marking tools are all that are needed. They are therefore the first 'proper' joint that most beginners attempt.

The principle is simple enough – corresponding holes are drilled in the

offset

angled

correct

Figure 126 Problems with bolt holes.

mating surfaces, then a dowel (a wooden peg) is inserted, with glue, to form the joint. However, drilling holes for a dowelled joint is the most demanding drilling task that will be encountered. Both the accuracy of the start point of the hole and its perpendicularity are vital to the success of this joint – if either is slightly 'out', then the joint will simply not close up. A variety of accessories are available to aid in both the marking out and drilling of dowel holes, but they all have their drawbacks and the best are very expensive. The advice given in the chapter on techniques will, if followed, take care of the perpendicularity of the holes, but marking out the start points calls for a foolproof strategy. One such approach is to mark out and drill one half of the joint, then to place 'dowel points' in the holes. When the second half of the joint is offered up to the first, the points leave an impression where the matching holes are to be drilled. A variation of this which requires no special equipment is to mark out the first set of holes on one of the mating surfaces, then tap in panel pins part way. Next, clip off the heads with pincers leaving sharp points projecting about 3mm from the surface.

USE DOWELS FOR:

Very light structural joints, edge-to-edge joining and where the joint must be hidden.

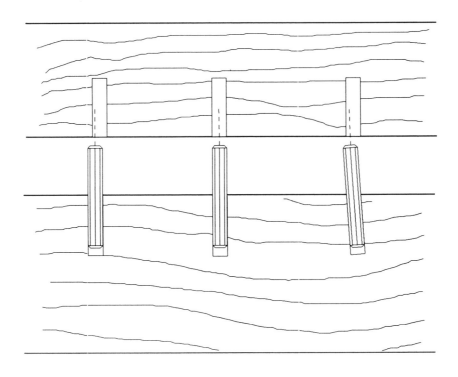

Figure 127 Dowel hole drilling.

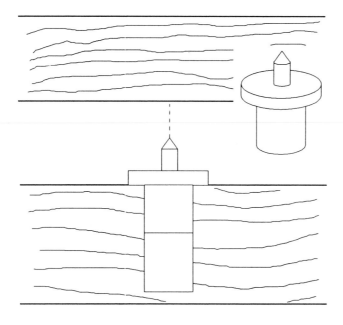

Figure 128 Using dowel points.

When the second part of the joint is pressed against the first, pin pricks will be made which correspond exactly with the pin holes in the first part. Remove the pins, and drill both parts.

Never use a mains power drill for dowel holes as they are not controllable enough – even a cordless drill should not be used for this without practice. Place the point of the bit in the marked hole and start to drill slowly, being careful not to let the bit slip at the start of the hole. It is a good idea to slightly countersink the

Figure 129 Marking dowel holes with panel pins.

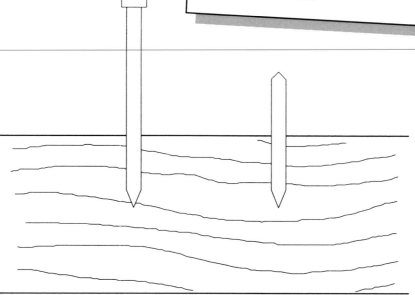

DO NOT USE DOWELS FOR:

Medium or heavy structural joints, joints where there are tension stresses.

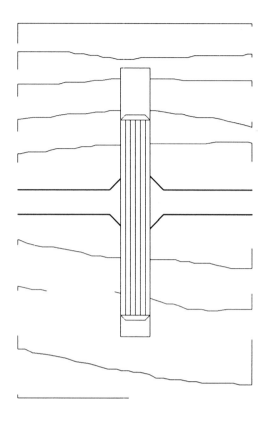

Figure 130 Countersinking dowel holes.

holes after they are drilled, as this allows the dowels to ease their way in, and will accommodate the inevitable squeezed out glue.

Unless ready-made dowels (which will be fluted) are used, it is necessary to cut a groove along the length of the dowel to allow the glue to squeeze out. If this is not done, the hydraulic pressure created by forcing the dowel into the glue-filled hole will stop the joint from closing and in extreme cases can actually split the wood. Clamping pressure is applied to the joint while it dries.

MORTISE AND TENON JOINTS

The mainstay of structural woodworking, there are many variations of the mortise and tenon. Used for making all kinds of framing joint where components meet at right angles, this joint has excellent resistance to compression and shear stresses, very good resistance to torsion, and if pegged has good resistance to tension.

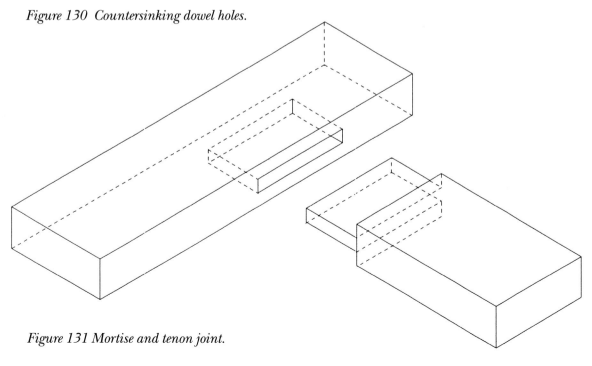

Figure 131 Mortise and tenon joint.

Variations include dismantleable types that can be used for structures which may need to be taken apart and for those which are prefabricated for assembly on site.

Mortise and tenon joints can be made with a few tools but require careful setting out and cutting. The principle is that a square tenon is formed at the end of one piece of wood and a matching socket cut into the face or edge of another. When assembled, the joint will, if made correctly, not only locate and hold the components together but will maintain the shape of the frame or structure. Before considering the various types we will look at the basic techniques involved in cutting this joint, as they are common to all.

Marking Out

Cutting a hole in a piece of wood weakens it, so the thickness of the mortise (and therefore that of the tenon) should be no more than one-third that of the piece into which it is cut. As a chisel is used for this process, it makes good sense to match the

thickness to that of your nearest chisel – so if the wood is 1¾in thick and you have a half-inch chisel, your tenons should be ½in thick even though this is slightly less than the prescribed one-third.

Mark the shoulders of the tenons and the width of the mortise using a square and a marking knife. Remember that the critical length measurement of a piece which is tenoned at both ends is the distance between the shoulders – not the ends of the tenons. Having done this, set a mortise gauge (*see* Chapter 4 on tools) to the width of your chosen chisel, then centre the gauge to the wood. Using this gauge, mark the thickness of the mortise and tenon on both halves of the joint.

Cutting the Mortise

The mortise is cut before the tenon, as it is easier to adjust the tenon to fit than the mortise. Use a lip-and-spur or an auger

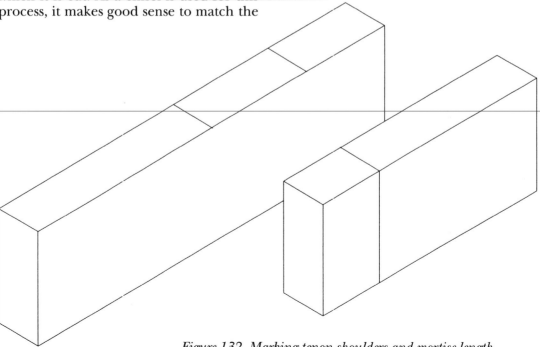

Figure 132 Marking tenon shoulders and mortise length.

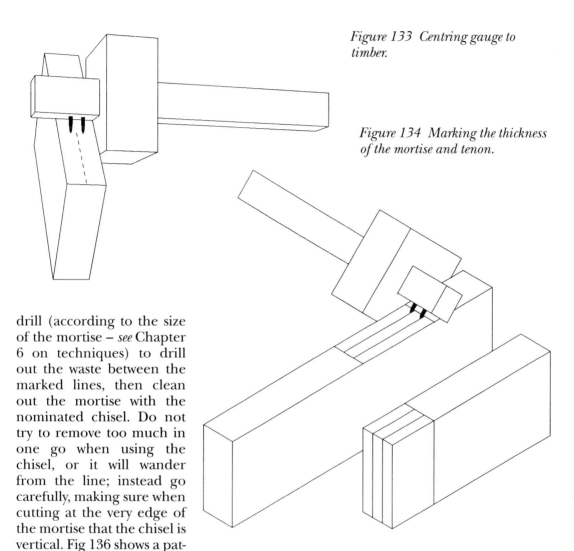

Figure 133 Centring gauge to timber.

Figure 134 Marking the thickness of the mortise and tenon.

drill (according to the size of the mortise – *see* Chapter 6 on techniques) to drill out the waste between the marked lines, then clean out the mortise with the nominated chisel. Do not try to remove too much in one go when using the chisel, or it will wander from the line; instead go carefully, making sure when cutting at the very edge of the mortise that the chisel is vertical. Fig 136 shows a pattern of chisel cuts which should ensure that control is maintained. If you are cutting a mortise for a 'through tenon' then work half way through from each side. This is for two reasons: first, it is important that the walls of the mortise are perpendicular to the face and edge, and secondly, breaking through from one side will make a mess of the other.

Figure 135 Drilling out waste.

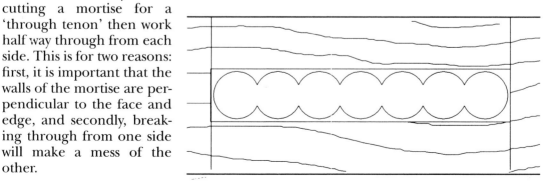

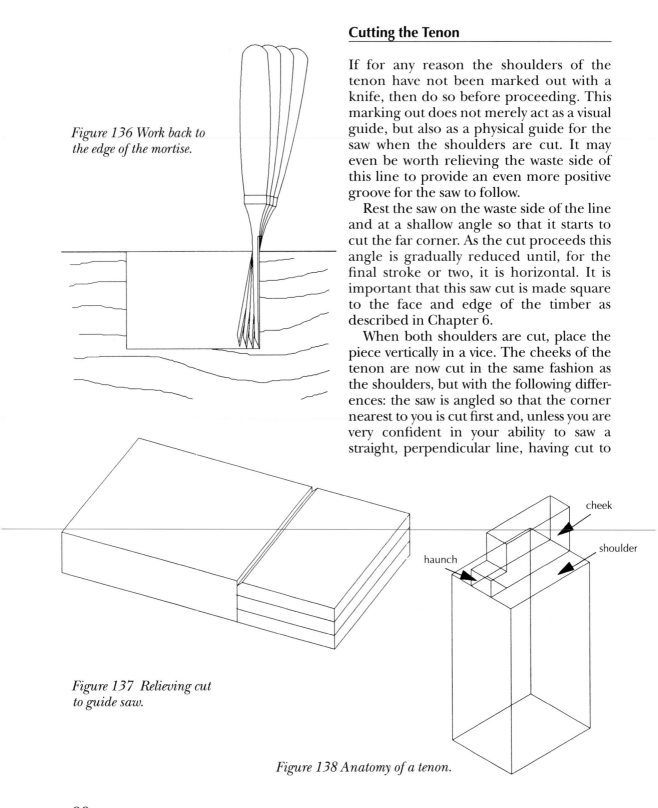

Figure 136 Work back to the edge of the mortise.

Cutting the Tenon

If for any reason the shoulders of the tenon have not been marked out with a knife, then do so before proceeding. This marking out does not merely act as a visual guide, but also as a physical guide for the saw when the shoulders are cut. It may even be worth relieving the waste side of this line to provide an even more positive groove for the saw to follow.

Rest the saw on the waste side of the line and at a shallow angle so that it starts to cut the far corner. As the cut proceeds this angle is gradually reduced until, for the final stroke or two, it is horizontal. It is important that this saw cut is made square to the face and edge of the timber as described in Chapter 6.

When both shoulders are cut, place the piece vertically in a vice. The cheeks of the tenon are now cut in the same fashion as the shoulders, but with the following differences: the saw is angled so that the corner nearest to you is cut first and, unless you are very confident in your ability to saw a straight, perpendicular line, having cut to

Figure 137 Relieving cut to guide saw.

cheek

shoulder

haunch

Figure 138 Anatomy of a tenon.

the far corner the piece is turned in the vice and the cut completed from the other side.

When both cheeks are sawn, test the tenon for fit in the mortise. Do not aim for a joint so tight that it has to be forced together. If there is not room for the glue, the joint will split when it is clamped up. A firm sliding fit is what we are looking for here and any tightness should be in the width of the tenon rather than the thickness. If this description of the process seems too simple to be true, it is because it is a simple joint. That isn't to say that things cannot go wrong. Generally a badly fitting tenon can be recovered by trimming and packing out, but sometimes what seemed like a set of well-cut joints will, when the piece is assembled, cause a distortion of the

structure. In the same way as a properly cut mortise and tenon will hold a structure square and true, a badly cut example will stubbornly do the opposite. The classic example of this is shown in Fig 140. Here a frame is twisted by a tenon that, though well-fitting, has been cut at an angle. This can be recovered by trimming and packing out, but as usual prevention is better than cure – take care when marking out, and practice sawing straight lines on a piece of scrap before attacking the work.

VARIATIONS OF MORTISE AND TENON JOINTS

The two main types of this joint are the through and the stopped tenon (Figure 141). The choice between the two is to an extent cosmetic (a stopped tenon does not show when the joint is closed) but there are structural considerations.

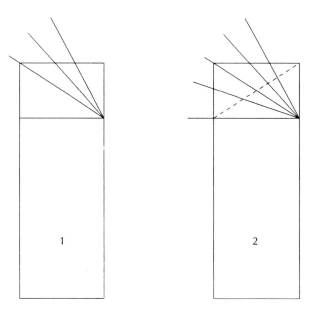

Figure 139 Sawing order for tenon cheeks.

Figure 140 Frame twisted by angled mortise.

A major advantage of the through tenon is that it can easily be wedged to tighten the joint. To do this, make two saw cuts along the length of the tenon, and hammer in wedges when the joint is together. Be careful that this hammering does not force the joint apart – it is best to leave the clamps on until the wedges are fully inserted. There are drawbacks, though, in that a through tenon means that the mortised part is weakened by having a hole cut all the way through it and the exposed end grain of the tenon is an opportunity for water to get in.

Stopped tenons are, as mentioned above, neater as the joint is not visible when closed. The mortised part will be stronger and less likely to split (through weathering as much as through the effect of stresses) as there is no exposed hole. Wedging this form of the joint is more difficult to achieve though, as the wedges must be inserted loosely before the joint is closed and pushed home by the bottom of the mortise when clamping pressure is applied. A fine judgement is needed to avoid the wedges stopping the joint from quite closing, based on the length of the wedges, their thickness and the compressibility of the timber. Sometimes the mortised piece is simply too large in section for a through tenon to be used, in which case a wedged, stopped tenon is the only option.

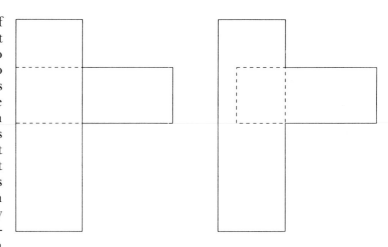

Figure 141 Through and stopped tenons.

Figure 142 Wedging tenons (below).

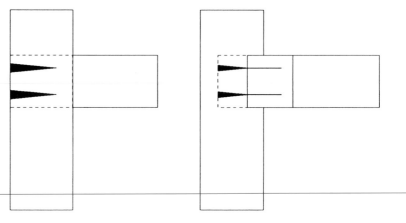

Drawboring

This technique may be applied to both through and stopped tenons and will both help to close the joint and hold it together in use, taking the place of an adhesive. One or two corresponding sets of holes are drilled through both the tenon and the sides of the mortised piece, offset in such a way as when a slightly tapered peg is hammered through it will pull the joint tight. These pegs are then sawn and planed

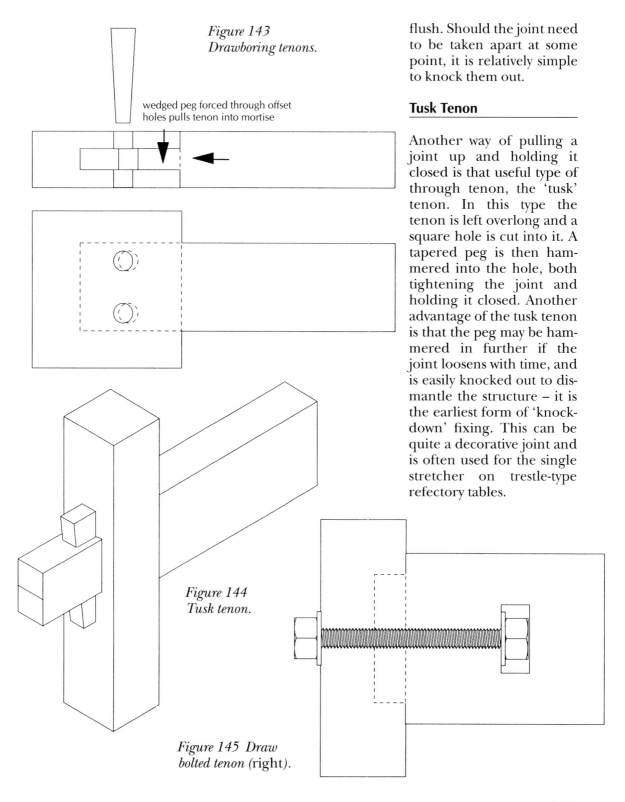

Figure 143
Drawboring tenons.

wedged peg forced through offset
holes pulls tenon into mortise

Figure 144
Tusk tenon.

*Figure 145 Draw
bolted tenon (right).*

flush. Should the joint need to be taken apart at some point, it is relatively simple to knock them out.

Tusk Tenon

Another way of pulling a joint up and holding it closed is that useful type of through tenon, the 'tusk' tenon. In this type the tenon is left overlong and a square hole is cut into it. A tapered peg is then hammered into the hole, both tightening the joint and holding it closed. Another advantage of the tusk tenon is that the peg may be hammered in further if the joint loosens with time, and is easily knocked out to dismantle the structure – it is the earliest form of 'knockdown' fixing. This can be quite a decorative joint and is often used for the single stretcher on trestle-type refectory tables.

Draw Bolted Tenon

Another dismantleable mortise and tenon joint, this uses a nut and bolt to tighten and hold closed a stopped tenon. It is especially useful if short ('stub') tenons must be used. First a stopped mortise and tenon joint is made in the usual way. A hole is then drilled through the end of the mortise and along the tenoned piece to accommodate a bolt. The nut is held in a slot (or a stopped hole if the piece is very thick) cut into the tenoned piece. When the bolt is tightened, so is the joint. Like the tusk tenon, the bolt may be tightened if the joint becomes loose or taken out to enable the structure to be disassembled.

The above are different ways of holding a through or stopped tenon in place – the actual type of tenon is also subject to variation according to the circumstances. The following types can be made in either through or stopped form and held together with any of the techniques already mentioned.

Haunched Tenon

Used where a tenon cannot be the full width of the tenoned piece, generally because the mortise is situated too near an end – at the top of a table leg, for example – and the tenon would be unrestrained. In this situation the width of the mortise and tenon is reduced, but for a short, shallow section to stop the tenoned piece from twisting.

Barefaced Tenon

Used where the tenoned piece is thinner than the mortised section but must be flush with its face, to avoid an over thin tenon. This joint is slightly easier to produce as

Figure 146
Haunched tenon.

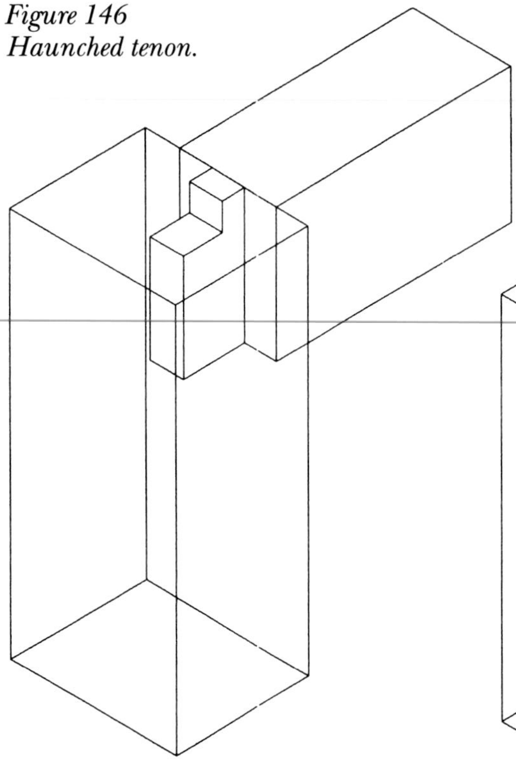

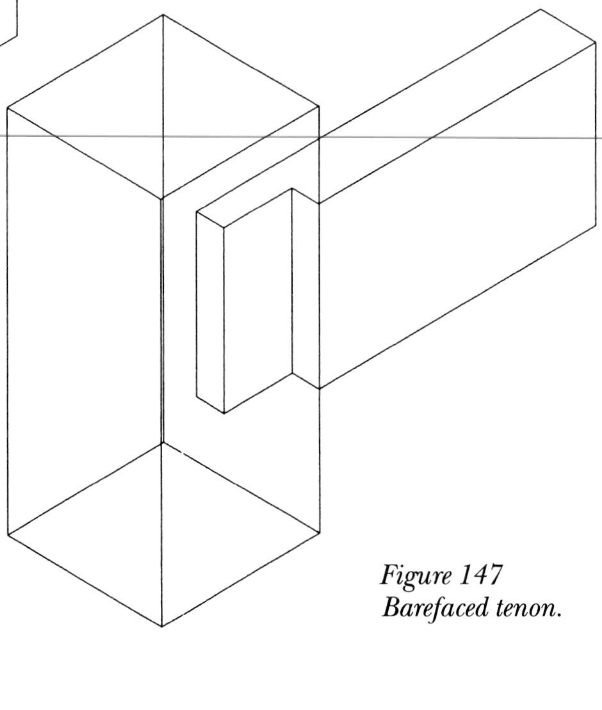

Figure 147
Barefaced tenon.

of shrinkage may be mitigated by reducing the effective width of the mortise and tenon, by making two or more smaller tenons rather than one wide one. A shallow haunch-like section is left between the tenons to prevent twisting or cupping.

Mitred Tenon

This allows two tenoned components to be mortised into a third at right angles to each other, but at the same point. Typical

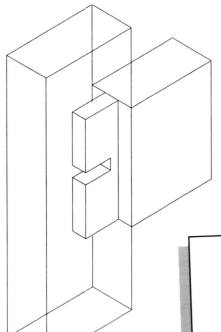

Figure 148 Double tenon.

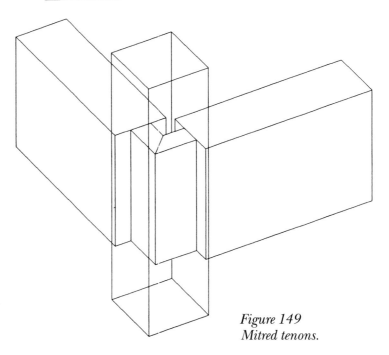

USE TENONS FOR:

All structural joints, framing, joining horizontal components to vertical, where torsion stresses are present.

only one tenon cheek has to be sawn.

Double Tenon

As mentioned previously, the tightness of a mortise and tenon joint should be in its width, holding the structure firmly in square. Unfortunately wood shrinks most in its width (for a full explanation, *see* Chapter 3 on wood). If a very wide piece has to be tenoned, any subsequent shrinkage will cause the tenon to become loose in the mortise threatening the security of the structure. The effects

*Figure 149
Mitred tenons.*

examples are rails tenoned into chair or table legs. Both sets of mortises and tenons are cut in the usual way, then the ends of the tenons are mitred to allow both to extend the full depth of the mortises.

BRIDLE JOINTS

The bridle joint is a sort of reversed tenon, with a slot being cut in the end of one piece to correspond with a reduced section on the other. It has very good resistance to compression, some resistance to shear, some resistance to torsion and little resistance to tension.

This is a relatively easy joint to make, following a similar process to that set out for tenons. Two forms of this joint are commonly used, the corner bridle and the 'T' bridle. The corner bridle is

DO NOT USE TENONS FOR:

Very light structures such as trellises, in which instance a quicker alternative will do just as well.

USE BRIDLE JOINTS FOR:

Light framing, joining vertical components to horizontal, where compression stresses are present.

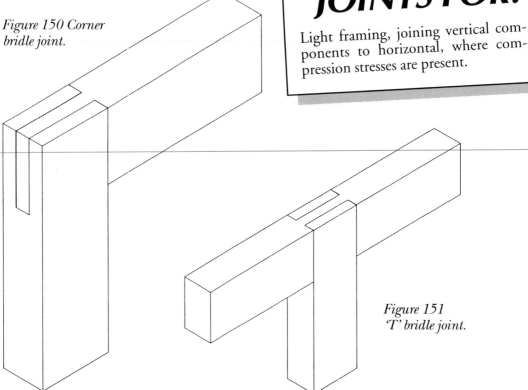

Figure 150 Corner bridle joint.

Figure 151 'T' bridle joint.

DO NOT USE BRIDLE JOINTS FOR:

Heavily stressed structures, unless the stress is compression.

useful for making light frames, but should not be relied on for structural framing. The 'T' bridle is a handy joint for placing vertical supports along a horizontal component, and providing that any stress is compression (a downward force on the horizontal piece) then it is very strong.

HALVING JOINTS

A simple all-wood joint, in which half the thickness of each component is removed allowing a flush overlap. It is used for light framing and for joints where components cross over each other, or meet at an angle. Resistance to stresses varies according to the specific type, but usually this is a locating joint requiring reinforcement (such as bolting) if used for structural purposes.

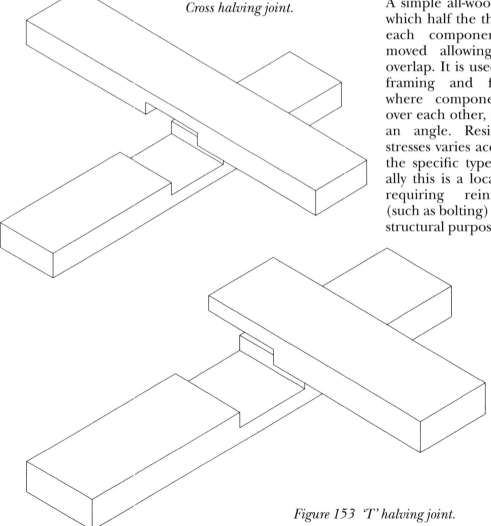

Figure 152
Cross halving joint.

Figure 153 'T' halving joint.

All that is required in the way of tools for this joint are measuring and marking equipment, a saw and a chisel. Procedure is similarly uncomplicated as each part of the joint is little more than half a tenon. The halving joint is unequalled as a means of dealing with components which cross over each other at any angle. To mark out simply lay one component onto the other, marking the overlap lines with a knife. Saw half way through each piece on the waste side of these lines, then remove the waste with a chisel. A waterproof adhesive will hold this type of joint together quite well and it may be reinforced with nails, screws or bolts according to the scale of the piece. 'T'

USE HALVING JOINTS FOR:

Light structural joints, very light framing, cross over joints.

DO NOT USE HALVING JOINTS FOR:

Medium or heavy structural joints, joints where there are tension stresses (unless the dovetail form is used).

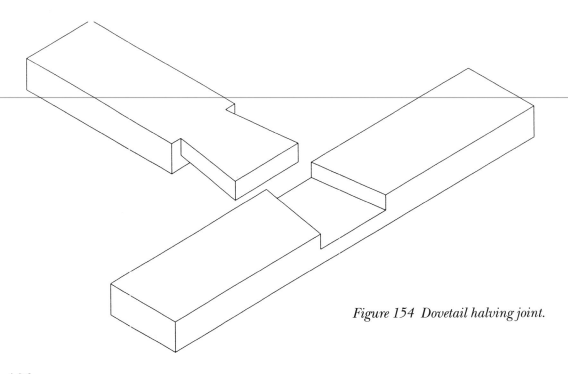

Figure 154 Dovetail halving joint.

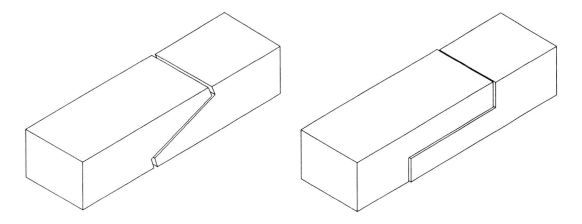

Figure 155 Notched scarf joint.

Figure 156 Simple scarf joint.

halvings are dealt with in the same way, but as one piece has a single shoulder it is less secure than the cross halving. A further variation which overcomes this problem is the dovetail halving which has the unusual property of resistance to tension (pulling) forces. Cut the dovetail shape on the end first, then mark round it with a knife to guide the saw when cutting the second part. If this type of halving joint is reinforced with a screw or bolt, then it is very secure.

SCARF JOINTS

All of the joints discussed so far are for joining wood at right angles, edge to edge or at an intersection. Where two pieces of wood have to be joined end to end, making one longer piece, a scarf joint is used. It is important to recognize that the best scarf joint in the world is much weaker than unjointed timber and so if one is used treat the resulting piece carefully.

The square cut ends of two pieces of wood present no opportunity for joining, so a section of long grain timber must be created. In its simplest example this takes the form of two diagonal cuts which can be glued and screwed or bolted together.

It is difficult to line this joint up though, as the two pieces are able to slip, so a more sophisticated form incorporates two notches which act as stops. These diagonal cuts are quite difficult to achieve and so the example shown in figure 156 may be a more realizable alternative.

There are, of course, many other types and variations of joints – dovetailing alone would merit a chapter – but these are the main groups applicable to garden furniture and amongst them will be found a solution to any jointing problem. They all rely on accuracy in marking out and cutting, but this is not difficult if it is approached carefully and enough time is allowed. Resist the temptation to take short cuts to hurry the process along, as this inevitably results in corrective work which probably takes longer than doing the job properly in the first place. Perhaps the best spent time of all is that spent thinking about the job before it is started – imagine the process first and potential problems can be headed off before they arise. Imagine the consequences of using a particular joint for a situation, ask yourself 'what if...' and success is much more likely.

 eight

Construction

We have already discussed the materials, fixings and fittings, tools, work space, techniques and joints likely to be used in the making of garden furniture. Most of the background information is in place and all that remains is to put all these things together and make something!

I hope that I have been able to show that in woodworking there are many ways to skin a cat and precisely what materials and techniques you use for each project depend on both the type of furniture being made and the experience and facilities of the maker. In illustrating the business of construction though, we will depart from this flexible approach in order to highlight the characteristics of each type of jointing method. It should be borne in mind, therefore, that the following examples are not necessarily recommended approaches, but theoretical models.

STRUCTURES

Before looking at individual approaches, the general principle of building structures should be considered. The types of structures covered in this book are all free-standing (that is; not supported by another structure, such as a building) and mostly load-bearing (benches and tables). They are certainly intended to withstand the buffeting of the wind. If the materials are chosen wisely and appropriate joints selected and made properly, then the chances of the structure falling apart are remote. Even if all of these criteria are met, however, it may still collapse under load and the culprit here is an effect known as 'racking'. This term is used to describe the distortion of a frame or structure by lateral forces, so that a square becomes a parallelogram. When this happens the joints are weakened and then… over it goes.

To illustrate this effect, try joining four pieces of wood with a nail at each corner, making a square frame. Pushing in almost any direction except exactly perpendicular to the centre of a side will cause the frame to collapse. Now nail a further piece

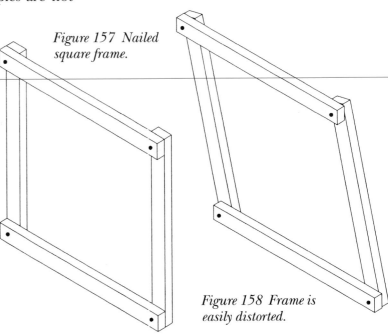

Figure 157 Nailed square frame.

Figure 158 Frame is easily distorted.

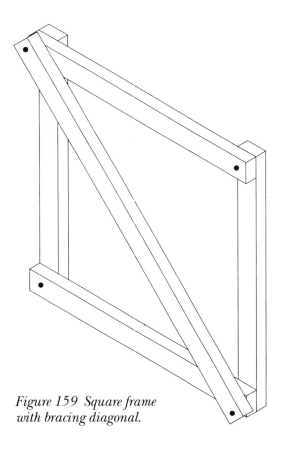

*Figure 159 Square frame
with bracing diagonal.*

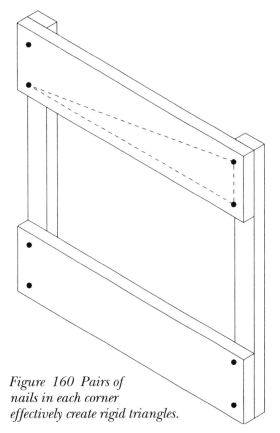

*Figure 160 Pairs of
nails in each corner
effectively create rigid triangles.*

of wood across the diagonal and try pushing again. You will find that it is impossible to distort the frame now that it has diagonal bracing. This is because a triangle has been introduced – and triangles are not collapsible. This is why roofs remain rigid and why so many square structures are built with diagonal bracing.

It is not necessary to include diagonal braces to introduce a triangle into your structure – if the collapsible frame in Figure 157 had been made with wider timber and two nails at each corner, then the nails would form a triangle and prevent the frame from collapsing. The wider the timber, and the further apart the nails, the more rigid the structure – and the less stress is placed on the joints.

A NAILED CONSTRUCTION

Everyone should have access to the facilities needed for building something with nails. Nails should not be used for the sole means of effecting structural joints and this means that in some cases we will have to create a simple mechanical joint which can then be held in place with nails. A saw and a chisel will be needed for this.

As nailing is an 'ad hoc' jointing method, let's also use an 'ad hoc' material – timber in the round, with or without bark. This implies a rustic style, so a seat of the type shown in Figure 161 will do very well as an exercise.

Reference to previous chapters tells us that the first job is to prepare a cutting list

Figure 161 Rustic seat.

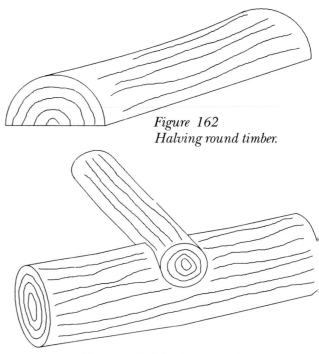

Figure 162
Halving round timber.

Figure 163 Notching round timber.

and cut to length all our components. As this is a rustic-style piece, the timber requires no further processing other than some pieces being halved along their length, so we can get straight on with making the joints.

Joints are all about restricting movement and round things are prone to rolling. There are three ways of dealing with this when constructing from timber in the round, the first being to flatten one side of the timber, and the second being to cut a notch for it to sit in. The third method, a combination of these, is to cut a halved joint. In the example shown, the seat rails are 'hung' onto the sides of the legs – this is a joint in 'shear' (*see* joints, Chapter 7) so they are halved to give a good mechanical joint which takes the weight, and nailed through to hold them in place. Onto these rails are nailed the seat slats which are

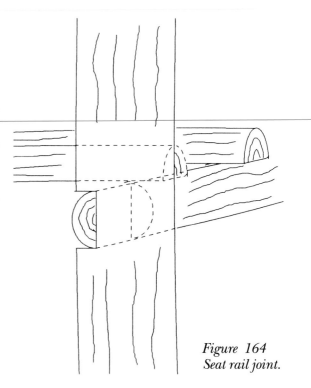

Figure 164
Seat rail joint.

they are halved into the back legs to add stiffness to the structure. To resist side-to-side movement, diagonal cross-braces can be added to the back (either nailed or flattened and nailed).

If you allow an hour or so for cutting the components to length and a generous three hours for cutting the joints and nailing, two of these seats could be made in a day, leaving the other half of the weekend to be spent sitting on them!

A SCREWED CONSTRUCTION

Given that a screw is just an improved nail, the structure shown in the previous example could just as easily be made using screws. However, it would be more usual to use screws with planed timber and so we will look at a more formal piece. The bench shown in Figure 165 has a very similar framing to the rustic chair, but as square, planed timber does not roll and screws will pull a joint tight, there is even

A simple trellis with stapled joints.

halved. These components' joints are in 'compression', so all they need is to be restrained from rolling. This is achieved by flattening one side, and nailing them onto the rails – two nails are used per joint, as a single nail would allow pivoting. Likewise the back slats are flattened on one side and nailed, as they are not stressed. The arms of the seat are flattened and nailed onto the top of the front legs, but at the back

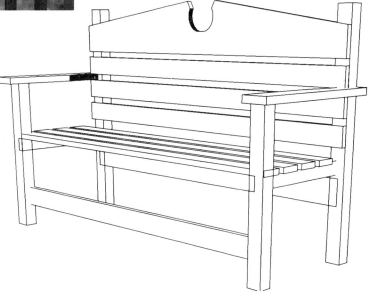

Figure 165 A bench.

less work to do. The two ends should be made up first. Cut neat, tight fitting housings for the seat rail and also for the rear of the shaped arm. To make life easier, the arm can be fitted before it is shaped, making accurate measuring and positioning a simpler business, then removed, shaped and refitted. The rail and arm are then screwed in place (the front of the arm is screwed down into the front leg) with two screws per joint – to resist racking.

A bench, being much wider than a chair, is more prone to sideways stresses and so a front and rear stretcher will be fitted, again into neatly cut housings. The rear stretcher is quite deep to offer more resistance to racking, but set high up so as not to appear clumsy. The slats for the seat and back are then screwed in place, again with two screws per joint.

The nice thing about screwing slats to a seat rail or back is that they can easily be made to follow a more comfortable, curved profile, by simply shaping the component to which they are screwed. A little trial and error may be necessary to arrive at the most comfortable shape, but the bench may be disassembled for alterations without too much trouble. Seats should be higher at the front, and backs should fall away to the top. A touch of elegance can be added by shaping the top slat of the back as shown – a simple operation which adds greatly to the bench's visual appeal.

A BOLTED CONSTRUCTION

Bolts are generally used for heavy-duty structures and those which are assembled on site. Therefore a pergola seems appropriate. These originate with the Romans (the name gives it away), who built very long examples so that they could race their horses through them in the shade. I would guess that few people nowadays will build them for such a purpose, but it is true that they may be made to any length

Figure 166 Seat and back angles of a bench.

by simply repeating the elements. The pergola in Figure 167 has four elements, which is very suitable for a short walk between different areas of the garden (through a vegetable plot, for example) or perhaps hamster racing.

The easily obtainable, preservative-treated four-by-two (any builder's merchant will have this in stock) will do very well for this project. The upright posts should be anchored firmly in the ground, the four at the outer corners (at least) being set in concrete, or into fence post anchors. Between these posts a horizontal member is coach bolted to each side, protruding at the ends and finishing with an oblique cut. Across the top are bolted crosspieces with the same oblique-cut ends. Stiffness is provided by the diagonal

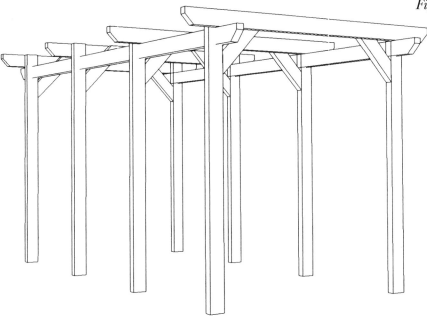

Figure 167 A pergola.

brackets which should be coach-screwed in position and can be fitted either inside the structure, or outside to provide a wider overhang – the projecting horizontal members are perfect for hanging baskets.

A TENONED CONSTRUCTION

The example shown for screwed construction could, of course, be made with mortise and tenon joints for the rails and stretchers. This would make no difference to the design of the piece or its use, but would look neater and probably last longer. The tenoned joint is the staple diet of joiners and is equally at home when used for the stretcher of a chair as it is for the rails of a panelled door, the component parts of a lych gate or the timber framing of a Tudor house.

As an example of tenoning in action then, a framed and panelled construction

Bench made with mortise and tenon and screwed joints.

113

Arm and seat slats screwed in position then plugged.

The end of a mortise in a seat rail (below).

is very appropriate, preferably smaller than a house but larger than a chair. How about a gazebo? Like the pergola, these can be made in any size from junior to garden party by either making the frames and panels bigger and/or making more of them.

A gazebo is intended to provide a shelter in which one might sit or stand to admire a view – a sort of palladian bus shelter – although in the modern garden they are more usually used to provide a view in themselves, or to obscure one (the compost heap is nicely out of sight behind a gazebo). Our example is a very modest one, yet should still add to the garden rather than detract from it. The frames are, of course, mortised and tenoned with an additional rail at just above knee height to allow for two different types of panel infill. The lower panel is formed from diagonally arranged boarding – tongue and groove – to provide a solid 'look' to the structure.

As a rule all structures should appear heavier at the bottom, otherwise they look unbalanced and flimsy. The direction of the boarding should alternate from one adjacent panel to the next, giving a herringbone effect, starting from the centre outwards to ensure symmetry. The upper panels are filled with a trellis so that the interior of the gazebo will not be too dark and gloomy. Climbing or trailing plants will add to the picture. There is nothing to stop us from placing chairs or a bench inside – the earlier examples, for instance – indeed building in a seat is especially easy by the simple expedient of suspending a slatted bench seat between the two sides. If this is done then the panels at the back should either be solid tongue and groove or the mid-rail higher, providing a more solid backrest.

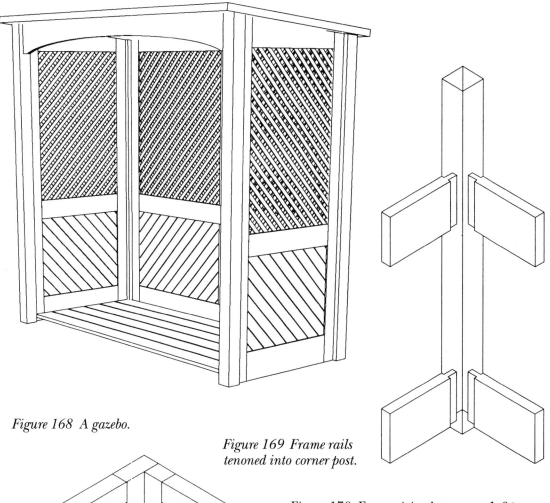

Figure 168 A gazebo.

Figure 169 Frame rails
tenoned into corner post.

Figure 170 Frames joined at corner (left).

There are three ways of approaching the construction of this piece; and they have to do with the treatment of the corners. Perhaps the more 'correct' method is to tenon the rails of both the sides and back into a corner post. This has the merit of keeping the components to a minimum and the structure visually simple. It also means that the job of assembly is more of a challenge, and would pretty much dictate that it must take place on site – unless you feel untroubled at the prospect of carrying the complete gazebo to its intended location.

The second method involves making up the side and back panels as separate frames which are then joined at the corners.

back frame, of course. The fall (or slope) of the roof need not be very great as it is quite small in area and the gazebo is unlikely to be occupied for very long in heavy rain or snow – the trellis sides will see to that! It is simply achieved by making the back panels shorter than the front posts; the side panels being made full height and cut to the fall afterwards.

The frames themselves are of a straightforward mortise and tenoned construction – refer to Chapter 7 on joints for details of cutting these. There is the business of fitting the panels to be considered, however. This may be handled as we would if fitting glass into a window frame; by cutting a rebate into the section from which the frames are made. This complicates the jointing somewhat as the shoulders of the tenons must be offset into the rebate, so if you would rather

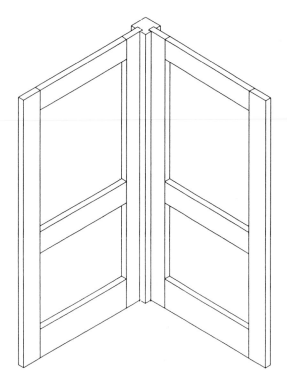

Figure 171 Frames grooved into corner post.

However, there is something 'not quite right' about this and it means that the frames must be of unnecessarily heavy section timber throughout. The third method allows for the frames to be of a reasonable section, individually portable to the location and for the structure to look 'right'. This involves using posts at each of the four corners between which the frames are fixed, thus resulting in a light, strong and elegant structure.

If this approach is followed, then the roof is also a good deal easier to deal with. A horizontal member can be fixed between the front posts (fitted to the inside, housing joints will do for this) onto which the front of the boards (or board) which make up the roof may be fixed. At the back they are fixed to the top of the

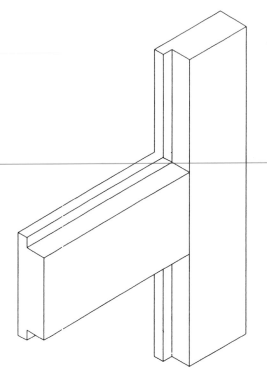

Figure 172 Frames from rebated section.

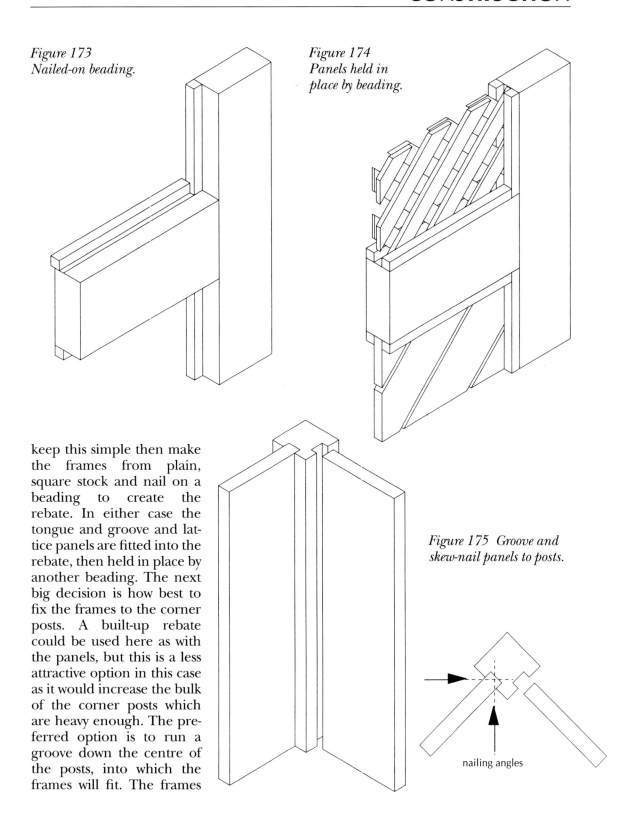

Figure 173
Nailed-on beading.

Figure 174
Panels held in
place by beading.

Figure 175 Groove and
skew-nail panels to posts.

nailing angles

keep this simple then make
the frames from plain,
square stock and nail on a
beading to create the
rebate. In either case the
tongue and groove and lat-
tice panels are fitted into the
rebate, then held in place by
another beading. The next
big decision is how best to
fix the frames to the corner
posts. A built-up rebate
could be used here as with
the panels, but this is a less
attractive option in this case
as it would increase the bulk
of the corner posts which
are heavy enough. The pre-
ferred option is to run a
groove down the centre of
the posts, into which the
frames will fit. The frames

can be fixed into these grooves by skew-nailing as shown, which will do the job more than adequately. If you wish to keep your options open as regards the future disassembly of the piece, then screwing through the posts into the frames instead of skew-nailing will allow this.

You will probably want to fit a floor to the structure, unless it is to be placed on paving stones or gravel. Slats are the solution again, as they will allow water to escape and reduce the build-up of mud from wellington boots. Fix a fairly heavy horizontal member across the front posts and another across the back, at their base – bolts here, I think. The slats will be fixed onto the top of these, running from front to back. This keeps them short, which means that they need not be of too heavy a section.

The roof can be as simple or as complicated as you like. A single piece of exterior grade plywood will do on its own if well sealed, or it may have roofing felt applied. Shiplap boards would also look nice, especially from the inside, and would be easy to fit. While we are weathering the structure, the lifespan of the frames will be lengthened if we fit weatherboards to their bases. Weatherboards are generally found at the bottom of exterior doors, and their function is to take the water that runs down the door away from it at the bottom, depositing it as a drip a couple of inches away. Figure 176 shows a weatherboard in section and the route taken by water. They are available as a ready-made section either in soft or hardwood from most builder's merchants and are so cheap that it is not really worth making our own. They are simply cut to length and screwed in place – from the inside if possible, as shown on the diagram, or with plugged holes if from the outside.

The decorative possibilities of a gazebo are endless – who could resist shaping the front roof-support, for example. Let yourself go here, as it is a frivolous structure and needn't be sombre – add as many twiddly bits as you like.

A TUSK-TENONED CONSTRUCTION

I will nail my colours to the mast here and now – this is my favourite method of jointing garden furniture. It satisfies all of the requirements; glue is not needed, it may be disassembled for storage or transporting, and if the joints become loose then a tap on the wedge-shaped peg will tighten everything up again.

The other aspect of tusk-tenoning which appeals to me is the extemporary nature of the joint. Since no adhesives, clamps or metal fittings are necessary it is possible to walk up to a few boards of timber with some simple tools and a couple of hours later stand back and survey a finished piece. As seating is such a primary form of garden furniture I will illustrate this approach with a simple four-plank bench. However, the principle is so versatile that it may be applied to almost any structure.

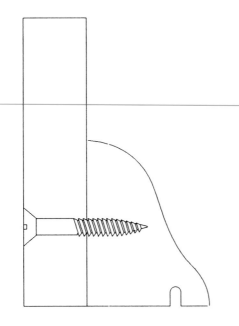

Figure 176 Weatherboard section.

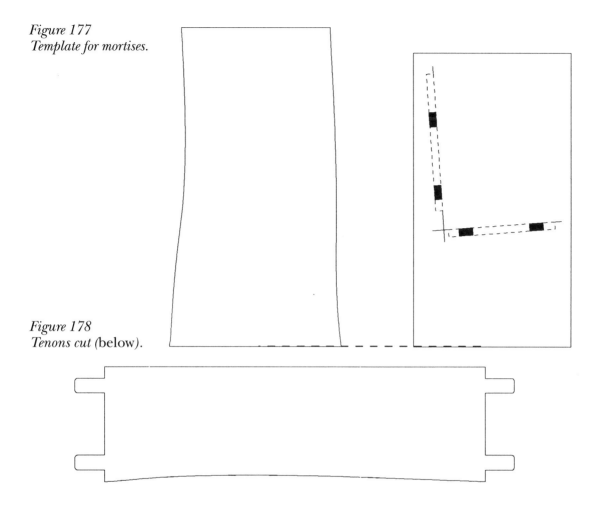

Figure 177
Template for mortises.

Figure 178
Tenons cut (below).

A native timber, bought waney-edged in wide boards, will suit this project best, and sweet chestnut with its natural resistance to rotting, ease of working and light weight will do best of all. Oak will serve, but in this instance should be viewed as a substitute.

One board sawn in two across its width makes the ends and another sawn in two along its length forms the seat and back. One face of the seat and back planks should be planed or belt sanded smooth, but no further preparation of the timber is needed. Prepare a template showing the angle of the seat and back in relation to the ground line. To calculate the most comfortable height and angle for seat and back, just measure a chair that you find easy to sit in.

Mark the position of the mortises onto the template – they should be a couple of inches in from each side of the seat and back – these can then be cut out of the template, allowing the positions to be marked through onto the sides. Cut the mortises with whatever tools are available; they should be neat but an exact fit is not essential as we are not gluing these joints. A router is probably the ideal tool for the job, as this will plunge into the timber and remove most of the waste leaving rounded corners to be squared off with a chisel. It will be found, though, that as good a job can be done with a drill, cutting several holes and once again finishing off with a chisel.

Having cut the mortises, transfer their positions to the seat and back. Again the most basic of tools will cut the tenons, a jigsaw is ideal but a tenon saw and a coping saw will soon have the tenons established. Be careful that enough length is left on the tenons for the peg holes to be cut – in sweet chestnut, for example, at least 40mm should remain once these secondary mortises are taken out. If the thickness of the sides (through which the tenons must pass) is a typical 30mm, allow a further 30mm for the mortise and 40mm remaining, making a tenon length of 100mm.

Make sure that the inner edge of the peg mortise is well inside the thickness of the bench sides. This joint works by the action of the wedge-shaped peg drawing the tenon tight in the mortise, and the peg must not become tight in its own mortise before this happens. Test the joints for fit and trim as necessary. When satisfied, cut eight wedged pegs. Too steep an angle on the pegs will make them prone to working loose, so it is better to make them longer than necessary

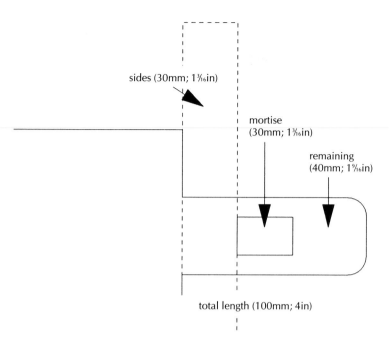

sides (30mm; 1³⁄₁₆in)

mortise (30mm; 1³⁄₁₆in)

remaining (40mm; 1⁹⁄₁₆in)

total length (100mm; 4in)

Figure 179 Secondary mortise.

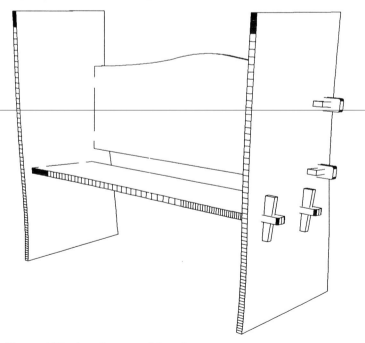

Figure 180 A tusk-tenoned bench.

and cut to a shallow angle. When the pegs are first knocked in they can be marked for length, popped out, trimmed and knocked back in.

At this stage the bench may be assembled. It is important to sand all sharp edges, as we are using waney-edged timber which is noted for its splinter-giving ability. An orbital power sander of some kind is ideal for rubbing over any corner or edge, but of course hand sanding will do – it just takes a little longer.

And that's it. Sweet chestnut will survive quite happily with no preservative treatment at all, but the bench will look nicer if given a couple of coats of Danish or linseed oil.

A HALVED CONSTRUCTION

Earlier in this book I have been quite rude about the standard-issue picnic bench. This is because the typical example, often seen in pub gardens and so on, is cunningly designed to be seriously unbalanced unless the occupants are evenly distributed on each side – and remain so. Most of us will have experienced the effect of someone standing up on one side, causing the whole structure to tip suddenly to the other. This is due to the seat of the bench extending beyond the feet and may be avoided by the simple expedient of keeping the seat within the 'footprint' of the bench. The picnic bench has some advantages after all, in that

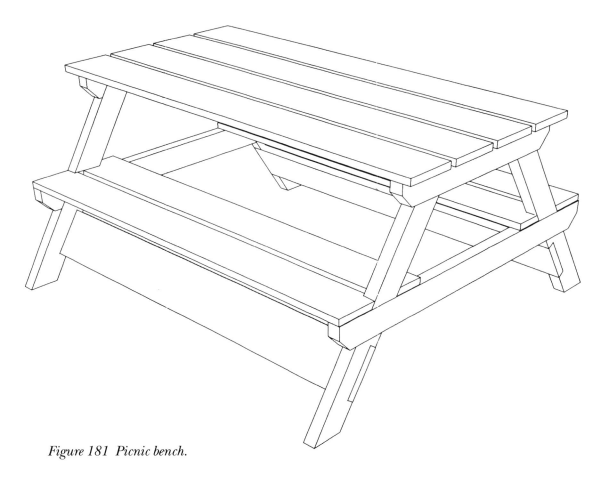

Figure 181 Picnic bench.

CONSTRUCTION

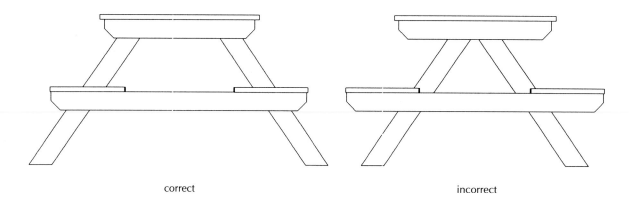

correct   incorrect

Figure 182 A stable bench.

a single unit provides both seating and a table, so properly designed it can be worthy of a place in the garden.

In essence these items consist of two trestles joined by the table top and bench seats. The trestles are especially suited to being constructed with halving joints and derive their stiffness by the shear resistance inherent in the cross-halved joint and the non-collapsibility of the included triangles. A fairly heavy section timber should be chosen both for weight (which adds stability) and to allow for the stock removal incurred when cutting halvings. As a picnic bench is a fairly utilitarian piece of garden furniture, prepared softwood is probably the most appropriate choice of timber, although hardwood may be used. Softwood will have to be very well treated with preservative as the design encourages standing water to remain on the surfaces. The exposed end grain will require special attention.

The joints are quite simple in themselves and reference to the drawing should be all that is needed (along with reference to the chapters on techniques and joints) to undertake this piece. Remember when cutting housing joints that the tightness of the shoulders is the critical factor in creating a rigid structure – the best way to ensure this is to lay one piece on top of the other and mark along its sides with a knife. Cut inside this knifed line and all should be well. The end trestles are the load bearing elements and should be made first, then connected by the rails which are there to resist racking – these are housed into the trestles below the seat and fixed between them below the top. The table top and bench seats are simply screwed in position.

Preservatives and Finishes

PRESERVATION

The object of preservative treatment is to slow down the combined assault made on exterior timbers by the weather, insects and fungi. Water is the main enemy and will pave the way for further damage by other agents. If your furniture is to live outside it will be subject to a high moisture content for most of the year whether it is raining or not.

All preservation is penetrating, in that the medium is absorbed to some degree by the timber. How well the timber is penetrated depends on the method, the timber and the medium. If you buy ready prepared timber it has possibly been immersed or vacuum treated, but at home brushing or spraying the preservative are usually the only practicable methods. There are a large number of products available, but unfortunately the manufacturers do not all use the same terminology to describe them, making comparison difficult – this becomes particularly confusing where brand names are involved. I have concentrated on the main suspension mediums here in an effort to overcome this.

Tanalized

If your wood is tanalized, the preservation is permanent and you will only have saw cuts and drilled holes to attend to. If you do not 'patch' the preservative barrier where it has been penetrated in this way, you have made a bridge over which moisture and fungi will march, eventually undermining all of your subsequent good work. This is true of all preservative treatments. Tanalized timber is completely safe when dry and is harmless to plants and animals. As it is a permanent treatment, it is a good choice for those parts of a structure in direct contact with the ground, such as fence posts. It can be finished with stain, paint or varnish, although the slightly greenish tinge will probably lead you to stain or paint it. You may choose to buy tanalized timber for the posts of a pergola, and use a cheaper timber for the cross pieces and treat them yourself, although this may not be cheaper in the long term. It is not impossible to persuade a timber merchant with tanalizing facilities to add a few pieces of your own to the pot, although using tanalized timber usually means buying it in that state.

Creosote

Creosote, made from tar oil, is by far the cheapest and most common preservative. Treated wood is often an orangey-brown colour, although it can be darker. It is poisonous to plants, so for *in situ* application they must be covered with polythene. Creosote is also messy to use and a skin irritant, so protective clothing (particularly for the hands) must be worn. It is not a permanent treatment, requiring reapplication every few years. It is also difficult to overpaint due to its chemical composition. It is, however, as already stated, pretty cheap.

Organic Solvent-based Products

Often based on white spirit, these work by fungicidal and insecticidal means and although odorous when wet the smell disappears after drying. Because of the solvent they penetrate wood well and can be overpainted providing that they have no additional water-repellent properties. They are also available with an incorporated wood stain, making the product both a preservative and decorative treatment which is valuable as a time saver. They can be toxic to vegetation so be careful to choose a horticultural-grade formulation for safe use with plants. The treatment is not permanent and requires application every few years.

Water-based Products

These products do not penetrate as well as organic solvent-based types, but have no odour and are much cleaner to use (the brushes can be washed out in water). They are also easily overpainted. Sometimes a water-repellent and wood dye are incorporated, making them an all-in-one product particularly suitable for finishing oily woods like teak which eventually reject oil-based paints. Because of the comparatively limited protection they offer, they are more suitable for timber which is not in contact with the ground, although adequate for benches and tables on hard standing.

Oils

I am including oil in this section; although it is often used as a finish, it is also a penetrating medium and as such has some preservative properties.

Danish oil is very popular these days for both interior and exterior use, and is more than a little trendy. Danish oil has much to commend it. Application is a nonchalant business, it is applied with either a rag or brush, left for fifteen minutes or so and then wiped off. Do this a few times once every six months or so, and a powerfully water resistant and otherwise protective

finish will result. Danish oil does form a skin if too much is applied, as drying agents are added to the mix which also contains Tung oil. Like all oils it will darken wood – already dark red hardwoods like Iroko become almost black – but can be used to treat timbers which resist penetrating preservatives.

A nice thin oil to apply, teak oil is a good all round treatment for exterior timbers. Very dark, it is also rather expensive and must have lost ground to Danish oil. Use nothing else on teak, of course.

Linseed oil is available in two varieties: boiled and raw. The difference? Boiled linseed oil forms a skin not unlike that of an oil-based paint, making it a popular choice for waterproofing canvas, but not necessarily wood. The raw oil has been used for many years (not just on cricket bats) as a protective treatment, and has acquitted itself well. Oak especially seems to benefit from this treatment, retaining its colour rather than becoming silvery-grey with weathering. It takes longer to dry than Danish oil, which is superseding it.

DECORATIVE FINISHES

Surface finishes can be divided into the two categories of opaque (paint) and transparent (varnish). Both of these oil-based products lie on the surface of the wood and act as a sealant, trapping moisture underneath, which eventually leads to cracking and blistering of the finish. Maintenance will require removal by sanding or burning off before new coats can be applied.

Microporous Finishes

Microporous varieties of paint and varnish have been developed to allow moisture to evaporate and the wood to 'breathe'; they are primarily for use on planed timber. Usually a two-coat treatment, they are most effective when applied to bare wood, or to wood whose previous finish has been thoroughly removed, but as they may have no preservative qualities it is necessary to also use one of the treatments already discussed. There are a wide range of colours and wood stains available in this category. Maintenance is often limited to cleaning and application of a further coat.

Remember that unless you want the furniture to be the focal point of the garden, it is best to keep to neutral colours, or natural wood grain. Garden furniture is often painted white, but remember that this colour will draw the eye and also make things appear nearer to the viewer, while blue tones help to create an illusion of distance. Naturally weathered hardwoods like teak, oak and chestnut, will turn a silvery grey in less than six months, a colour which blends with any planting and never looks out of place.

Oil and Stain

Some finishes are penetrating, like oil and stain, both of which will leave the grain of your wood visible. Oiling will protect your furniture from immediate weathering but will need applying at least once a year. Oil darkens the surface each time it is applied and can also attract dirt. Where it is used on seating, a drying off period is required so that clothes are not stained on contact.

Once your timber is oiled you will not be able to change your mind about the finish (although Danish oil can be overpainted) and therefore careful consideration should be given to the pros and cons before reaching for the tin. As preservative can be bought with stain already added, it is often unnecessary to purchase this separately. Ultraviolet light from the sun can affect the permanence of some stains so check that the product includes an inhibitor before purchasing – one description of these is 'light-fast'. Waxing exterior woodwork is not worthwhile and like oil will prevent application of subsequent finishes.

APPLICATION

Brushes

If you are using creosote you will need to keep a separate brush solely for it, as you will not be able to use it for any other purpose afterwards. Therefore use either an old brush or a cheap one – if you can find one cheap enough to throw away afterwards, so much the better, as it will save you from storing a very smelly item.

Other products are not so injurious to your equipment and any paint finish will benefit from application with a good quality brush. Use brushes where spraying will damage or mark surrounding plants or other structures, and for products with low viscosity.

Spray

Liquid preservative or wood stain is easily applied with a garden sprayer and for trellis and other elaborate structures spraying is by far the quickest option. If there is only a small area to be treated, you could use one of the very cheap hand held trigger-operated sprays. The electric 'blat gun' type of powered sprayer gives an appalling finish when used for paint, but will pump a large volume of solvent-based preservative in no time. When spraying anything, though, wear adequate respiratory protection (check the product's packaging for warnings). Many of the more effective preservative treatments are highly dangerous when they come into contact with the delicate membranes in the respiratory tract.

Cloth

Only really effective for use with well planed and sanded timber, but useful for oil and stains to ensure an even finish on important work. The oil is applied first to the cloth and then to the wood. A coarsely woven, slightly absorbent cloth works best, seeming to push the oil or stain into the grain. This type of cloth will also drag surplus oil from the surface, avoiding pools and runs. A well-used bar towel is the optimum material, in fact, so cultivate a good relationship with your local publican (if you have not already done so).

Working Space

If you had problems finding a place to build your furniture, then finishing it will raise more. Ventilation is usually the main concern and it is much safer to wait for a fine day so that you can work outside even if it is cold. It is not a good idea to work in windy conditions if you are using sprays, as the vapour will be blown back onto you, or if you are using paint then wind blown debris will behave as if the wet paint is magnetic! When you apply any of these finishes remember to protect your hands, eyes and clothes, as well as the surface on which you are working. Preservative which is liquid will easily splash or run onto plants or you, and will make hideous marks on a lawn if the work is laid there for treatment. Use a sheet of polythene, or even bin liners if there is no wind. Large pieces like panels of trellis may better be finished *in situ*, unless this raises problems of reaching all of the parts. Preservative has to be applied at all stages of the making process to ensure that no saw cuts or drill holes are left bare, paying particular attention to end grain. It is not necessary for your timber to be planed to accept a finish; all of the preservatives and stains can be applied to rough-sawn timber. Remember, though, that colours will appear darker on rough-sawn timber as the 'hairy' surface is highly absorbent. Always test pigmented products on scrap timber, as different timbers will give a variety of effects with the same product.

INDEX

INDEX